⚐ **W9-CLL-434**

The
FULL FORCE
of Your Ideas

MASTERING THE SCIENCE OF PERSUASION

CONTRIBUTING AUTHORS

KEVIN DALEY

PAM ERB-MELVILLE

WAYNE TURMEL

DIANE BIEGERT

LEE VELTA

COMMUNISPOND

www.communispond.com

Published by
Communispond
52 Vanderbilt Avenue, 7th Floor
New York, NY 10017
800-529-5925
www.communispond.com

ISBN 0-9761569-0-3

Trademarks and Service Marks are the property of their owners.

Library of Congress Control Number: 2004098345

CONTENTS

A Note on Style

Outmoded English usage specifies the masculine form of a pronoun (he, him, his) when the antecedent could be either gender. But this implies something about the relative status of genders that doesn't deserve support in this book. The logical way to make the language more gender-equitable is to replace "he" with "he or she." Replacing one word with three, however, is inelegant in the writing and often awkward in the reading. Our solution has been to use the feminine form sometimes and the masculine form other times. If the change from one to the other sometimes seems abrupt, we hope you nevertheless prefer it to the reinforcement of aging (and dying, we hope) stereotypes.

The Authors

"The Audience Remained as if Stunned"

EVERY AMERICAN SCHOOLCHILD KNOWS THAT PATRICK HENRY made a speech in which he said, "Give me liberty, or give me death." We all remember this line as a stirring patriotic moment. More than two centuries after the American Revolution, however, it is easy to lose sight of that quotable line as a moment of persuasion. Patrick Henry's speech was one of the few moments in human history in which someone moved a body of men to do something decisive, dangerous, and (as many saw it) opposed to their own interests. To get the full impact of this extraordinary event, we need to understand a little of its background.

Things were tense in the American colonies in 1775. In the spring of the previous year, the English Parliament had passed a series of restrictive laws and even took away territory from some of the larger colonies to give to Canada. The colonies then convened a meeting called the First Continental Congress, which declared its opposition to these laws and others. British newspapers published editorials describing the colonial actions as treason. The punishment for treason in 1775 was death by hanging.

In February 1775, however, a provincial congress in Massachusetts adopted defensive preparations against the 14 regiments of British troops garrisoned there. The English Parliament declared Massachusetts in a state of rebellion.

In this atmosphere, the colony of Virginia held its political convention in March, 1775. The delegates, most of them plantation owners with a great deal at risk in the event of war, were eager to cool down some of the anti-British sentiment brewing there out of sympathy for Massachusetts. They seized hopefully on overtures made by the British to preserve the peace with twelve colonies that had not rebelled.

One of the first orders of business in the Virginia Convention occurred when someone proposed a resolution promising every effort to repair deteriorating relations with the Crown. As the members of the convention debated this resolution, a delegate named Patrick Henry proposed an amendment to it. This amendment was actually a means of killing the resolution, for it called for the raising of a militia to defend Virginia, presumably from the forces of the Crown! The delegates then shifted to a debate on Henry's amendment, and when he took his turn, he made a brief speech:

> *No man thinks more highly than I do of the patriotism, as well as abilities, of the very worthy gentlemen who have just addressed the House. But different men often see the same subject in different lights; and, therefore, I hope it will not be thought disrespectful to those gentlemen if, entertaining as I do opinions of a character very opposite to theirs, I shall speak forth my sentiments freely and without reserve.*

"Without reserve" turned out to be an understatement.

"This is no time for ceremony," boomed Henry. "I consider it as nothing less than a question of freedom or slavery." Then he turned the tables on the British who accused the colonists of treason and declared that it would be treason to hold back his opinion at such a time. It would be, he said, "an act of disloyalty toward the Majesty of Heaven."

He insisted that those who wanted peace with Britain were deluding themselves. The behavior of Parliament for the past ten years had offered no evidence it was willing to allow any of the colonies the liberty they felt they deserved. When the colonies sent petitions for redress, he insisted, the British accepted them with a smile while planning even more coercion. "Suffer not yourselves to be betrayed with a kiss," he said. "Ask yourselves how this gracious reception of our petition comports with those warlike preparations which cover our waters and darken our land."

The time for argument and entreaties was past, he declared. "Sir," he said, "we have done everything that could be done to avert the storm which is now coming on. We have petitioned; we have remonstrated; we have supplicated; we have prostrated ourselves before the throne, and have implored its interposition to arrest the tyrannical hands of the ministry and Parliament." All efforts at peaceful reconciliation had been rebuffed. Every avenue of redress had been exhausted except one, he said. And the final alternative was to fight.

Then he took up the question of whether the colony was prepared for such a fight. Delay, he insisted, would only weaken them and give the British the opportunity to disarm them. And he was certain the colony was strong enough for the fight. "The millions of people," he intoned, "armed in the holy cause of liberty, and in such a country as that which we possess, are invincible by any force which our enemy can send against us." And the war, he said, was inevitable. "There is no retreat but in submission and slavery! Our chains are forged! Their clanking may be heard on the plains of Boston! The war is inevitable—and let it come! I repeat it, sir, let it come."

Then, as he built to the climax of his speech, he declaimed the conclusion that put him in the history books:

It is in vain, sir, to extenuate the matter. Gentlemen may cry, Peace, Peace— but there is no peace. The war is actually begun! The next gale that sweeps from the north will bring to our ears the clash of resounding arms! Our brethren are already in the field! Why stand we here idle? What is it that gentlemen wish? What would they have? Is life so dear, or peace so sweet, as to be purchased at the price of chains and slavery? Forbid it, Almighty God! I know not what course others may take; but as for me, give me liberty or give me death!

As he spoke the final sentence, Henry brandished an ivory letter opener, which he held above his chest, then brought it slowly down as if to stab himself. "After Henry sat down," wrote his biographer, "the audience remained for a brief time as if stunned."

Some may be tempted to write off Patrick Henry as a dead guy who is of little concern to people trying to live in the 21st century. But his "liberty or death" speech is a milestone in the science of persuasion.

Virginia was completely unprepared for he fight he was advocating, and his audience knew it. The colony's entire stock of munitions consisted of a little powder and a few muskets in Williamsburg. They would have to raise, arm, and train troops for defense. In addition, every man in that hall knew that taking up arms against the government was treason and liable to the severest punishment. Finally, the colony's leaders thought the British Crown was going to moderate its measures. There was every reason to try to cool things off. Rarely has a single speaker faced a more difficult audience to persuade. Yet Henry's speech caused the Virginia Convention to pass his resolution of resistance unanimously and to put him in command of the militia!

What do we know about the delivery of this speech, aside from the gesture with the letter opener? His biographer tells us there is no manuscript of the speech, and the traditional account that has come down to us today appears to include impromptu remarks. His biographer speculates that he made the speech with no more support than notes. So it is not only a great speech for us to read today. It had a great delivery, and it was well rehearsed.

By the standards of the day, it was understated. It was not witty, profound, or humorous. It ignored much of classical rhetoric. But it was a speech that changed people's minds, and it got a hall full of men to make a public commitment to a measure that defined them as traitors and subject to capital punishment. How often does that happen?

Patrick Henry was not a distinguished man. He was neither wealthy nor well-educated. But he knew how to persuade men to lay their lives on the line. He was a persuasion scientist. We hope you will never have to ask as much from an audience, but we think it is possible for you to learn the techniques that can move people to action, and that's what this book is about.

You can find the full text of Patrick Henry's speech, along with a number of other brief, persuasive speeches, in the appendix to this book. We suggest you read it after you have read this book and see how closely it adheres to the science of persuasion as we describe it.

PART I
The Science Of Persuasion

CHAPTER 1

The Science
of Persuasion

THE ENGLISH WORD PERSUADE PROBABLY CAME FROM the French word *persuader*, which today means to induce, convince, or satisfy and hasn't changed meaning very much in 600 years since it entered English.

The word did not gain currency until the 16th century. In 1513, the *Oxford English Dictionary* tells us, the word made one of its earliest appearances in written English, when Sir Thomas More used it in *The history of kyng Richard the third unfinished*: "The Quene being in this wise perswaded, such woorde sente vnto her sonne, and vnto her brother."

We don't know what persuaded the Queen to send word to her son and to her brother, but the sentence shows that persuasion inspired action. Nearly 500 years later, inspiring action is what we are after when we undertake to persuade someone.

According to *The Random House Dictionary of the English Language* (Second Edition), "persuade" has two meanings in modern American English:

1. to prevail on (a person) to do something, as by advising or urging

2. to induce to believe by appealing to reason or understanding; convince.

In fact, most people use the word to mean both things at once, for if you can get a person to believe a certain way, you can influence that person's behavior. And for our purposes in this book, we define persuasion as the act of using communication to change the attitude, belief, or point of view of another person without deceit.

You can see we are modifying the accepted definition. Most people would say it is possible to persuade someone deceitfully, and we admit that is true. But that's not what we're talking about in this book. We are going to examine legitimate persuasion.

Appealing to Reason

The dictionary suggests you can achieve persuasion by "appealing to reason." Certainly most businesspeople try to persuade that way—by straightforwardly stating an argument, presuming that once an audience sees something from the "proper" perspective, opinions will fall in line.

It would be nice if our professional lives were so ordered and logical.

But is the modern workplace a realm of order and logic? Anybody who has worked with other people knows what it means to have a fight-or-flight reaction in a business meeting. Someone is holding forth on "New Directions in Marketing for Legacy Products," and you can feel your heart rate increase. Your muscles tense, your palms perspire, you begin to breathe in short gulps, all your senses go on alert. Your body is behaving exactly as it would if you'd come face-to-face with a large predator. But no one here is threatening you. No one is armed. Why is your body acting like it expects to begin fighting for your life? The only thing that's happening is someone proposing to take away your department's role in the marketing of the company's most important products.

The truth is, "New Directions in Marketing for Legacy Products," depending on your responsibilities and your knowledge of others' intentions, can be as threatening to you as a saber-toothed tiger was to your ancestors.

Have you ever been grief-stricken by the discontinuation of a product? Angry when someone in the organization did not meet a commitment to you? Joyful about the successful completion of a project? The workplace is a cauldron of emotions, and the successful business professional recognizes those emotions, controls them in herself, and understands them in others.

An Emotional Process

And it's important to understand that, regardless of what the dictionary says, persuasion works by acting on the emotions, at least in part. When someone converts your point of view, it is often more than a minor adjustment based on a logical marshalling of arguments. You feel persuaded, and your commitment to the new point of view involves more than just your rational mind.

Most people assume that this emotional aspect makes the act of persuasion artistic, spiritual, or ineffable. For centuries, the techniques used by successful persuaders have been known as the art of persuasion.

But persuasion is not necessarily based on charisma, charm, inspiration, or any other magical quality. The techniques that great persuaders use are precise and quantifiable. Persuaders may, in fact, be artistic, but they are first and foremost scientists and technicians of the science of persuasion. This book is a review of that science.

It lays out the fundamental principles, and then it examines what effective persuasion looks like in light of these principles.

It considers persuasion in its three main venues: large groups, small groups, and virtual (which is the best word we can find to cover persuasion situations in which you're not face to face).

For some people, the idea of persuasion is related to that of manipulation. We believe nothing could be further from the truth. If you're looking for techniques of manipulation, we must tell you to look elsewhere. On the surface, persuasion and manipulation may resemble each other, but the manipulation of another person's point of view will last no longer than it takes the person to discover the manipulation. Persuasion, on the other hand, can last forever.

CHAPTER 2

The Principles
of Persuasion

PRINCIPLE #1
Every point of view is reasonable
to the person who holds it.

BAY AREA ACTION, AN ENVIRONMENTAL EDUCATION AND action
organization based in San Francisco, has a website where you can down-
load an "SUV ticket." It is a graphic designed to look like a parking ticket, and environmental activists can print it out and then leave it on an
SUV as a kind of "educational" exercise.

This ticket is good-natured when you read it closely: "I [the ticketer]
certify under penalty of perjury that I am not just being mean. I really
just want to help the poor soul who is owned by this vehicle." The ticket lists 12 possible "violations" the ticketer can check off, including:

- did not realize SUVs pollute more than twice as much as regular cars
- did not realize SUVs do not have the emission controls that cars do
- ego overruled environmental consciousness.

The SUV ticket may be funny and even a little charming, but it
should not be mistaken for an instrument of persuasion. A parking ticket is a tool of the police, and while it is friendlier than a baton or a pair
of handcuffs, it is nevertheless intimidating. And intimidation, even
mock intimidation, never persuaded anybody of anything. You can force
somebody to do something with intimidation, but you can't change a
person's mind with it.

Maybe after reading the ticket, the owner will have a chuckle and
enjoy the good-natured ribbing. But it's still safe to say Bay Area Action's
SUV ticket has not persuaded many SUV owners to give up their big
vehicles, and it has no doubt alienated some.

Why would someone not eagerly change her mind when we make her the butt of a joke or the target of intimidation? The answer seems ridiculously obvious when you ask it that way, but many of us still act as if we think we can change a person's mind by shouting in his face, ridiculing his beliefs, or hitting him with a pie.

SUVs may not be friendly to the environment, and they are increasingly recognized as a bad investment for our society. But the purchaser of any particular SUV might have good reasons for the deal, ranging from a good price to cargo space to a brother-in-law who sells them. And unless you're first willing to give the SUV purchaser credit for the possibility of behaving reasonably, all your arguments about gas mileage, emissions, and safety will fall on deaf ears.

The American culture wars of the past two decades have polarized a long and growing list of issues, including abortion, gay rights, prayer in school, sex education, and the teaching of evolution, to name a few. But have any of the culture warriors on either side of these many issues persuaded anyone? In fact, there has been so little conversion from one side to the other on any of these issues that you would be justified in thinking that the continued discussion is not intended to influence people's thinking but only to stir them up.

This is not the place for a sociological discussion of the culture wars, but it is self-evident that none of the participants is getting persuaded of anything, except perhaps a stronger attachment to their own position. The simple fact is that persuasion requires as much listening as talking, maybe more.

You cannot achieve the act of persuasion until you can exercise your imagination and put yourself in the other person's shoes. Putting yourself in another's position has two benefits for the act of persuasion. The first is that by understanding the other person's position, you respect the other person. She senses your respect, and this opens her to new ideas.

The second way it works is in promoting your curiosity about the other person's position. Your increased curiosity leads you to get information about the person's position, which can give you strategic insights for approaching the person. If you know, for example, that someone clings to an outmoded marketing plan because it gives his department influence or prestige in the organization, then you know that you're most likely to persuade him to adopt a new plan by developing one that gives his department influence or prestige in some other area, if not marketing.

There are often good reasons for confronting others, and there are even times when intimidation or ridicule is appropriate. So throw a pie if that's the form of communication that is required, but don't delude yourself into thinking you are going to persuade the pie's target to adopt a new point of view.

PRINCIPLE #2
Persuasion does not result from argument or debate.

Anyone who has lived through a U.S. presidential election is familiar with debates. A presidential debate generally goes like this: a moderator explains the rules, the candidates debate according to the rules, and commentators appear afterward to explain who won and who lost. Televised presidential debating dates from the election of 1960, when John F. Kennedy and Richard M. Nixon squared off for the cameras. Over 40 years' worth of debates since then has produced long rosters of debate winners and debate losers. But no debate has ever seen one candidate persuade another.

Debates are sporting events, and they are a healthy component of the dialogue that keeps democracy functional, but they are performed for the benefit of spectators. But it is doubtful that any debater, no matter how skilled, has ever gained from the audience (much less the other side!) that emotional commitment that results from persuasion.

Argument is debate's unruly sibling and is distinguished from it by a general lack of rules and moderation. Technical and legal arguments are more formal (and more productive), but everyday argument exists solely for scoring points. But there is no generally accepted point scale, so the outcome of an informal argument is usually difficult to ascertain.

Informal argument is performed in bars, homes, and cable television studios in order to create winners and losers. There is no procedure for deciding the outcome, however, and the "winner" is usually the participant with the loudest or the shrillest voice. An argument usually continues until one side gives up or it's time to cut to a commercial. And if you ask more than one spectator who won the argument, that question itself usually produces an argument.

Argument as practiced in the modern world can be energizing, it can be healthy, it can be entertaining. It cannot persuade. Losing an argument does not cause the emotional reversal we recognize as persuasion; it simply alters the form of the loser's resistance, converting it to humiliation, resentment, determination, or anger. Losing is a negative state, while being persuaded is a positive state. Most people will not acknowledge the loss of an argument, and those who do will usually qualify it: "You win, but I'm not convinced."

If Principle #1 tells us to respect the position of the person we seek to persuade, Principle #2 tells us that persuasion is a not a win-lose proposition. Persuasion is, in essence, a cooperative transaction. It results not in a winner and a loser, but in two winners. If you want to argue, go ahead and entertain yourself. But if you want to get someone to adopt a point of view, change an attitude, or enthusiastically embrace a behavior, avoid argument and persuade.

Everyone in business is familiar with the phenomenon of the winner who doesn't win. This is the person who forces a recommendation on an organization by "winning" an argument. Inevitably, however, the "losers" nurse their resentment and never fully embrace the recommendation or continue doing things the old way anyway. The result is usually far more punishing for the winner and the recommendation than losing the argument would have been.

In many ways, persuasion is the antithesis of argument. Where argument is all about using logic, reasoning, or intimidation to "win," persuasion is all about raising someone's receptivity to an idea and then helping him find a way to embrace it. You do this partly by modeling your commitment to and passion for the idea and partly by showing the other person how she will benefit from adopting your point of view. To persuade someone is to make a sale. The persuaded person doesn't always pay in money, but there's a cost (even if it's just in mental comfort) to giving up a position, point of view, or attitude with which you're comfortable. Your job, as the persuader, is to show the other person that the new position, point of view, or attitude is worth the cost.

Look at this way. How often have you seen a sales person argue with a prospect? It doesn't happen very often, because sales people who argue don't usually remain sales people for very long. Have you ever bought anything from someone who argued with you?

PRINCIPLE #3
A persuasion event begins
long before you utter a single word.

In the following chapters, you will learn how much preparation goes into an attempt at persuasion. You cannot realistically expect to persuade someone of something without a significant amount of prework.

The first description of preparation for persuasion may be in an account of the life of Demosthenes, an orator who lived in Athens in the fourth century, B.C. After being humiliated during a speech in the city assembly for "a weakness in his voice, a perplexed and indistinct utterance and a shortness of breath," Demosthenes was given some pointers on speaking and gesturing by an actor friend. It was a new style of oratory to him, but he decided it would bring him success. According to the biographer Plutarch:

Hereupon he built himself a place to study in underground... and hither he would come constantly every day to form his action, and to exercise his voice; and here he would continue, oftentimes without intermission, two or three months together, shaving one half of his head, that so for shame he might not go abroad, though he desired it ever so much.

Demosthenes prospered because in those days, one's reputation and even livelihood depended on one's ability to make an effective presentation—just as your livelihood and reputation depend on it. Don't for a moment think this has changed in the past 2,400 years!

By shaving half his head and locking himself in a basement, Demosthenes set a legendary standard for preparation for a presentation. But in fact, Plutarch only describes the persuader's final preparatory step—that of rehearsal. He omits the five critical steps that precede it:

- goal determination
- audience analysis
- identification of audience benefits
- gathering evidence
- preparation of visuals.

Projectors and flip charts were scarce in fourth-century Athens, and there is no documentary evidence that Demosthenes supported his speeches with visuals. But you can be certain he went through the other steps, because persuasion does not occur without them.

We would go so far as to say that, while rehearsal is fundamentally important, if you are effective in the other preparatory steps, you probably don't need to shave half your head and lock yourself in a basement to get ready for your persuasion event.

Many people in business lose sight of just how much of a performance is involved even in day-to-day work. Whether you're trying to make a sale, reorganize a division, or install a new procedure, you can't get buy-in without a decent performance. Everybody expects a good show and won't be persuaded without one. A good show requires a great deal of prep work, including (as Demosthenes would tell you, if he were here) intensive rehearsal.

When should you begin to prepare? Any time after immediately may be too late. You will need all the time you can get to determine what you want to achieve by your persuasion, gather information on your audience, and figure out how to align your goal with the audience's needs.

PRINCIPLE #4
Persuasion takes place in the mind and feelings of the persuaded, not the persuader.

As we described in Principle #1, every point of view is reasonable to the person holding it. Because we all believe our point of view is reasonable, we assume that if we can just get other people to see a matter the way we see it, they will adopt our point of view. This may be true in a general sense, but it's not a very productive way to look at the task of persuading. It causes us to focus on our own point of view, when the best way to get our point of view across is, paradoxically, to adopt the other person's point of view—so we can reconcile it with our persuasion goal.

Most people, when they attempt to communicate, focus their attention on themselves, planning what they will say next and reviewing progress on their agenda. This is a fine strategy if you're simply conveying information. For persuasion, however, you must focus your attention not on yourself but on your audience, because that's where your agenda is unfolding, whether you like it or not.

The paradox of persuasion is that you cannot convert another person to your point of view unless you give it up—at least long enough to understand the point of view of the person you're trying to persuade.

Communicating is not quite so simple as Aristotle supposed. In the fourth century B.C., he said communication has three components: speaker, speech, and audience. This simple model was all anyone needed for more than two millennia, although as new media (first print, then radio and television) gained in popularity, the components were relabeled "sender," "message," and "receiver."

But the past 60 years have seen the creation of more sophisticated models of communication that reflect both our increased understanding of human psychology and the rise of information theory. Today, most students of communication rely on the "convergence model." The convergence model describes communication not as a linear operation with a beginning and an ending, but as a continual process of interpretation and response leading to mutual understanding. In this model, meaning is not in the message the sender sends to the receiver. Meaning is something that happens between the sender and the receiver as a result of their interaction.

In a lot of everyday communications, such as "Please pass the salt," meaning is simple. And it doesn't make much difference whether you frame it as something sent by the sender to the receiver or something worked out cooperatively between them. The result is the same: the receiver passes the salt. But the convergence model gets more important as the message gets more complex, subtle, or important. The receiver's understanding depends, not just on what's in the message, but on the context in which he hears it, his own background, and his expectations.

As a persuader, you need to understand your audience so you can take advantage of their background and expectations. As we suggested in Principle #3, audience analysis is one of the critical steps in preparing to persuade. To get your meaning inside the head of another person, you need to understand how that person would benefit from adopting your meaning, and you need to understand the benefit from that person's point of view.

Your role as a persuader is that of a facilitator. The actual persuasion, strangely enough, is performed by the person being persuaded. Throughout most of human history, people have not understood this aspect of it, and have attributed persuasion to the talent or magic of the persuader. But you don't need some sort of magical talent to facilitate the process if you understand it. And understanding that people aren't persuaded so much as they persuade themselves is one of the keys to the science of persuasion.

PRINCIPLE #5
The more communication channels a persuader uses to convey the message, the greater the chance persuasion will take place.

In 1927, in a publication called *Printer's Ink*, Fred R. Barnard penned the immortal remark, "A picture is worth a thousand words." He called it "a Chinese proverb, so that people would take it seriously." But he needn't have bothered. Anyone who has ever encountered the remark has understood and adopted it. It has attained the status of a cliché, and like many clichés, it has the ring of utter truth.

Research has shown that adding graphics to text increases the learning of adults by about a third and that they remember more than 40% more of the contents of a document when it includes graphics. Visual communication is so effective that most business professionals wouldn't dream of making a presentation without a PowerPoint file to support their remarks.

To persuade, you should approach your audience through both their hearing and their vision. This means using visuals to illustrate, support, and amplify your remarks. Making a point graphically, with a chart or a picture, can be more effective than simply stating it. And doing both at the same time (we'll explain how in a later chapter) can dramatically increase the point's impact for anyone, regardless of their favored communication channel.

But there is a corollary to this principle that many would-be persuaders lose track of: your presentation is always more than what you say. If people absorb and process information through multiple communication channels, that means they are attending to those channels whether or not you are using them. They take in a lot of information about you just from looking at you. Albert Mehrabian, a UCLA professor, researched communications extensively to determine the impact of different kinds of information on audiences. In studies of inconsistent communication (in which the speaker's words don't match his or her body language), he estimated that the receiver takes 38% of meaning from how the speaker sounds, 55% from how the speaker looks, and only 7% from what the speaker says!

Mehrabian's findings mean that your audience probably attaches more importance to their interpretation of your posture, your mannerisms, and your facial expressions than they do to anything you tell them. From watching you, they gather information they use to make judgments about your sincerity, your credibility, and your intelligence. They can't help it. Human beings are virtually hard-wired to make these judgments. This is one of the reasons we have jury trials in the U.S. The jury trial is based on the proposition that people can judge things like sincerity and credibility by watching someone testify.

We will provide more detail on how to control the visual presentation of yourself in a later chapter. Just remember that persuasion is only 7% words. Even if your recommendation will solve the audience's biggest problem, even if it will let them go home earlier to their families every evening, even it if will provide them with wealth beyond their dreams, if you do no more than say it to them, they may not understand it. You must say it and show it, so you can approach them through two senses at once.

Let's just have a word on the other three senses. Most people have a favored sense, which is why some of us can learn to identify different kinds of wine faster than we can learn to identify different cars, or some us can learn to roller skate faster than we can learn the lyrics of popular songs. And some of us can learn song lyrics by hearing them while some of us must see them written out.

In most persuasion events, you will not have the chance to approach your audience through their senses of smell, taste, and feel. You can serve refreshments, but it may be difficult to find a way to make a connection between your persuasion goal and, say, a cheese danish. On the other hand, by covering all the sensory modes with your language ("visualize it this way…" "try this idea on for size…" "maybe this example will speak to you…"), you may be able to raise the receptivity of those who favor different senses. And that may be the only technique we have until Microsoft invents AromaPoint.

PRINCIPLE #6
Persuasion requires a persuader; visuals can never do more than support a persuasion event.

When you open Microsoft PowerPoint on your PC, the software invites you to create a "PowerPoint Presentation." This unfortunate nomenclature has crept into general usage, and you will often hear a PowerPoint user refer to a computer file as "my presentation." Nothing could be further from the truth. Your PowerPoint file is a PowerPoint file. Your presentation is nothing less than your presence, your remarks, and the impression you create before your audience. For better or worse, you are your presentation.

We have taken some pains to explain in the previous principle that it's important to persuade through as many senses as possible and to use visuals whenever you can. Visuals provide clarity to your ideas and sometimes they are able to make statements that are impossible to make verbally. But it's easy to go overboard. If your visuals incorporate a riot of colors, animations, music, fancy backgrounds, and trendy typefaces, you will draw your audience's attention away from yourself. No audience is ever going to be persuaded by your visuals.

In order to persuade an audience, you must not only dominate your visuals, you must control them. Be aware that every time a new slide goes up on the screen, it's news, and nothing attracts attention like news. Don't leave it to your audience to interpret the news; do it for them. As soon as a new visual appears on the screen, tell the audience what it means, and you will be the source of all knowledge on your topic. In a later chapter, we will give you specific techniques for management of visuals and interpreting them for your audience.

PRINCIPLE #7
Successful persuasion depends on the audience's trust in the persuader.

Have you ever been persuaded by a person you didn't trust? Sometimes we run into a person who says he has indeed been persuaded by someone he didn't trust. But probing invariably shows that the distrust followed or even preceded the actual persuasion and that at the moment of making up his mind, the persuaded trusted the persuader.

Social scientists define trust as a willingness to become vulnerable to another based on your positive expectation of that person's actions or intent. This definition reminds us that human beings give something up (i.e., defense) in the trust transaction because they expect something positive in return. That means to gain people's trust, you need to make them feel safe enough to lower their defenses and you need to convince them it will be worth it.

Those who have studied the phenomenon of trust say there are characteristics that tend to inspire it. That is, the more you observe these characteristics in another person, the more likely you are to trust that person.

The first of these characteristics is ability. We tend to put more trust in people who are knowledgeable, skilled, or competent. One of the reasons television commercials for hair restoration products use spokespeople in white lab coats is that a white lab coat suggests a person is a doctor or a scientist, and everybody knows doctors and scientists have a lot of training. This is not to suggest you should don a white lab coat the next time you attempt persuasion. But you should appear competent. That means being in command of the evidence you are using to persuade, and it means being in command of the equipment. Presenters who fumble with their slides or mishandle microphones are not generally persuaders.

The second characteristic is integrity. We tend to put more trust in people who abide by principles we find acceptable. And we form judgments about the integrity of others based on the consistency of their behavior, their honesty, their sense of fairness, and whether they act in accordance with what they say. The best way to demonstrate integrity is to be honest, consistent, and fair. This is especially true in a business organization, where your audience is likely to know you, at least by reputation.

The third characteristic is benevolence. We tend to put more trust in people who are concerned about our welfare. Benevolence is the most interesting trust-building characteristic because it generally takes the longest to establish. Human beings are often willing to assess ability and integrity by intuition, but benevolence requires harder information. So trust-building begins with ability and integrity and moves on to benevolence. We have all worked with people we've felt are concerned about us, and those are the people in the organization we tend to trust most.

Sometimes the audience's trust in the persuader is misplaced. In the book *Coercion: Why We Listen to What "They" Say*, Douglas Rushkoff tells the story of a high-pressure salesman named Mort, who sells a mechanical bed to an elderly couple:

> *By the time all three were gathered once again around the kitchen table, Mort had sold the wife on his company's best bed, but the husband was unsure. Time for an old trick he'd developed during his days on the used-car lot. He told the old man that he was down at the warehouse yesterday, where he saw two improperly labeled mattresses. Their serial numbers indicated that they were standard mattresses, but he could plainly see that they had heating units installed—an $800 value.*

Mort then made a call to his friend at the warehouse to find out the mattresses were still there, and reported back to his prospects that only one of them had been sold. The other was claimed by Mort's competitor for his customer. But if Mort could get a signed sale, the warehouse would release it to him.

Mort didn't tell his customers that all the mattresses came with a heating unit, and he let the husband's competitive spirit carry him away with the idea of taking the sale out from under Mort's competitor.

Mort went on to sell them a time payment plan, doubling their costs, on the strength of a series of complex calculations that "proved" they were saving an additional four percent. This is coercive selling and it's of a piece with the tactics employed in some boiler room telemarketing operations. Some sales people in these games are so expert at manipulating a prospect's feelings about himself that they can get a sale with no trust involved.

Another transaction that resembles persuasion but does not require trust is outright coercion, not every form of which requires an explicit threat. When you do something against your own judgment simply because the person who signs your paycheck tells you to do it, that's a form of coercion. It can be benign, as in the case of the supervisor who parcels out unpleasant assignments, or it can be malign, as when a manager compels a subordinate to falsify records or break the law.

PRINCIPLE #8
A persuasive message must be memorable, active, or meaningful.

In 1998, the journal *Philosophy and Literature* held a bad writing contest and awarded first prize to a single sentence that appeared in a scholarly article:

The move from a structuralist account in which capital is understood to structure social relations in relatively homologous ways to a view of hegemony in which power relations are subject to repetition, convergence, and rearticulation brought the question of temporality into the thinking of structure, and marked a shift from a form of Althusserian theory that takes structural totalities as theoretical objects to one in which the insights into the contingent possibility of structure inaugurate a renewed conception of hegemony as bound up with the contingent sites and strategies of the rearticulation of power.

Admittedly, the author of this sentence (Judith Miller, a scholar sometimes cited as "one of the ten smartest people on the planet") probably wasn't interested in persuading anyone—except the six or seven scholars stubbornly clinging to the old form of Althusserian theory. History does not record whether the message was successful with them. But this sentence—being unmemorable, inactive, and unmeaningful—is priceless as a bad example of persuasion.

Let's look at the three qualities of a persuasive message.

Memorable messages are always brief, and they are distinguished by a kind of poetry. There are numerous messages of persuasion that are so memorable they continue to have currency today, long after they ceased to mean anything:

"Fifty-four Forty or Fight!"

This message is so memorable that most schoolchildren can quote it. But few people know what it means. (It comes from a campaign promise made by James K. Polk in the 1844 presidential election.) Its rolling alliteration keeps it in mind today. It is memorable, but to modern hearers, it lacks meaning.

Active messages use active verbs and sweep us up in their momentum:
- Workers of the world, unite! (from *The Communist Manifesto*)
- Just do it (Nike advertising slogan)
- Don't leave home without it (American Express advertising slogan).

These are all active, although coming from advertising and propaganda, they don't carry very deep meaning. Whether or not they are memorable is debatable. Only one of them is comparable in age to "Fifty-four Forty or Fight," and it remains to be seen whether it will long survive the fall of Communism in the popular imagination.

Meaningful messages strike an emotional or intellectual cord that resonates in us, at least at the time they are uttered:
- Morning in America (Ronald Reagan campaign slogan)
- "I have a dream…" (from a speech by Rev. Martin Luther King, Jr.)
- Think small (a famous contrarian advertising slogan for Volkswagen).

These messages are all meaningful, but not particularly active. They are memorable, too, however, and that may be because they are still so meaningful.

And some messages manage to combine more than one of these qualities:
- Be all you can be (U.S. Army advertising slogan)
- "Ask not what your country can do for you; ask what you can for your country." (from the 1961 inaugural address of President John F. Kennedy)
- "The only thing we have to fear is fear itself." (from the first inaugural address of Franklin D. Roosevelt).

Regardless of how profound, moving, or poetic they are, persuasive messages tend to be simple. This is well understood by the professional persuaders in advertising. Advertising, which is one of the world's largest industries, employs hordes of people whose main job is to simplify messages. Advertising's stock in trade is the slogan—from the 16th century Scottish Gaelic "sluagh-ghairm." Sluagh means army or host, and gairm means cry. So the original meaning of slogan is "war cry." You can't get much simpler than a war cry.

To see how simplification works, consider the case of Stride Rite, a manufacturer of upmarket infant shoes. Stride Rite had no problem selling baby shoes to young mothers, since its product was widely viewed as high-quality, trustworthy, and expensive. But families tended to stop with a single pair of Stride Rites, and as the baby got older, they bought shoes that might not have the same quality or expense. Stride Rite hired Mullen Advertising to help it "re-position" its product. The new position for Stride Rite shoes was expressed with this mouthful:

> *Stride Rite is the brand that allows kids to embrace life's possibilities and adventures with confidence.*

Mullen Advertising then put all its creative resources to the task of expressing this position as simply as possible. In many, many person-hours of effort, the agency finally produced this slogan:

"Life's waiting. Let's go."™

What matters isn't so much that the slogan led to substantially increased sales (although it did), but that creative minds were able to reduce a 16-word, fairly abstract, statement to a four-word line that makes you want to get up out of your chair. Does Mullen Advertising know something about persuasion? You bet they do.

PRINCIPLE #9
Persuasion never occurs when the persuasion message is unclear.

It ought to be self-evident that a message incapable of being understood is incapable of persuading.

But some would-be persuaders haven't mastered the clarity principle. Page through almost any magazine, and you will eventually come across an advertisement that "almost" seems to make sense. We found one recently for a line of mattresses that bore the headline: "Felt but not seen." The illustration was a picture of a bed. There was other text that eventually explained that this mattress doesn't look any different than an ordinary mattress, but it incorporates space age materials that make it more comfortable. But the headline, by challenging the reader to puzzle out its meaning, works as provocation rather than persuasion.

The best persuaders make clarity look easy, but achieving it is labor-intensive, and it requires an effort of imagination. You must take the message you intend to communicate and imagine yourself hearing it for the first time with none of the associations you have built up around it over the course of working with it.

Here are a few of the signs that can alert you that your message may lack clarity:

- jargon
- wordiness
- vagueness
- ambiguity
- passive voice
- complex words
- conditionals (if-then) nested in other conditionals.

One of the best resources on clarity is a tiny book by William Strunk, Jr. and E. B. White. It is called *The Elements of Style*, and it has existed in various editions and formats since the 1930s. In addition to notes on usage, composition, form, and commonly misused words, it offers 21 rules of style, ranging from "place yourself in the background" to "prefer the standard to the offbeat." It has rescued countless communicators from incoherence.

We can't stress this principle enough. In business, there is a strong temptation to use dispassionate technical or professional language. We can feel that tendency even while we write this! But technical and professional language can be the enemy of persuasion, partly because it takes the passion out of communication, but mostly because it interferes with clarity. This is why the engineers and developers rarely write the documentation.

If you would persuade someone, invest the time up front to make your message as clear as you can possibly make it. Test it on people who have never heard it before you try to use it on the audience you want to persuade.

The Principles of Persuasion

PRINCIPLE #1
Every point of view is reasonable to the person who holds it.

PRINCIPLE #2
Persuasion does not result from argument or debate.

PRINCIPLE #3
A persuasion event begins long before
you utter a single word.

PRINCIPLE #4
Persuasion takes place in the mind and feelings of the
persuaded, not the persuader.

PRINCIPLE #5
The more communication channels a persuader uses to convey
the message, the greater the chance persuasion will take place.

PRINCIPLE #6
Persuasion requires a persuader; visuals can never do more than
support a persuasion event.

PRINCIPLE #7
Successful persuasion depends on the audience's
trust in the persuader.

PRINCIPLE #8
A persuasive message must be memorable, active, or meaningful.

PRINCIPLE #9
Persuasion never occurs when the persuasion
message is unclear.

PART II
Persuading Large Groups

CHAPTER 3

Controlling
Your Anxiety

IN APRIL, 2003, ACTOR JAMES GARNER GAVE A HALF MILLION dollars to the University of Oklahoma School of Drama. Garner, who is known to two generations of television viewers as the star of "Maverick" and "The Rockford Files," also made over 40 films and was nominated for an Academy Award in 1985. At the public ceremony to announce his gift to the School of Drama, he became slightly discomposed. Recovering, he said, "Strangely enough, I have a fear of public speaking." Garner went on to explain he never feared appearing in front of a camera "because I know I can always do it over."

A 2003 survey by The Aziz Corporation found that 100% of company directors in England believe good communication and presentation skills are essential for a successful business career. But more than 80% admitted to being fearful of making presentations, an increase over the 67% who admitted it the previous year.

As anyone who has cracked a book on presentations knows, *The People's Almanac Book of Lists*, first published in the 1970s, identified public speaking as one of the most common fears of modern Americans. It places just behind fear of snakes in some editions, but it places ahead of the fear of death in all of them. If you have no fear of public speaking, you're not only extremely unusual, but you've escaped a condition that plagued such legendary public speakers as Cicero, Benjamin Disraeli, and William Jennings Bryant.

Most people can talk comfortably with one to four people. But when the crowd reaches five or more, that's when fear of public speaking begins to kick in. That makes five people a neat dividing line between small and large groups. And since this chapter is about persuading large groups, we thought this was the appropriate place to take on fear of public speaking. If you're fearful of making a presentation to fewer than five people, there's probably something other than a fear of public speaking at work: fear about your career, holding on to your job, making the sale, getting the promotion, or whatever.

It seems for most people, however, addressing an audience of five or more people can cause butterflies in the stomach, or even profuse sweating and shortness of breath. Let's look at this fear so you can learn ways to manage it and become a better persuader.

Fear of Public Speaking

Anxiety about public speaking is not uncommon. If you need proof of this, just look around. Therapy designed to help people overcome their fear of public speaking is a growth industry. (Like many growth industries, it is filled with charlatans and scammers, but that's another story.) And 2001 even saw the news that one of these therapeutic organizations is now using virtual reality "therapy" and biofeedback. There are also hypnotists who will "cure" you of your fear, as well as psychotherapists and speech coaches.

But we think it's counterproductive to look at the fear of public speaking as a disorder needing treatment. Calling this anxiety "glossophobia" and "treating" people for it does a disservice to most of the "patients." If a public figure like James Garner betrays a fear of speaking to a roomful of students to whom he is making a gift of a half million dollars, can we consider this condition in any way pathological?

To say that someone who doesn't want to give a presentation has a fear of public speaking or suffers from glossophobia is like saying a shy person suffers from agoraphobia. But agoraphobia is a serious disorder and keeps a small number of people housebound. Shyness just gives people discomfort about meeting new people. There are people who suffer from glossophobia, and they are probably about as numerous as those suffering from agoraphobia, and they need treatment if they are going to realize the benefits of being effective persuaders. If you find yourself utterly disabled by your fear of public speaking, seeking treatment may be a good idea.

But nearly all human beings suffer nervousness and anxiety about getting up and speaking in public. Why would we not? Deep in our genes is the understanding that calling attention to ourselves in a group of people puts us at risk. If there is a pride of lions stalking a herd of wildebeest, we don't think the wildebeest that tries to stay in the center of the herd is suffering from any kind of pathology. Human beings aren't wildebeest, of course, but there was a time in our primordial past when most individuals did not want to be conspicuous in the possible presence of predators. Modern anxiety about calling attention to oneself through public speaking may be what's left of that fear.

We are not going to refer to a fear of public speaking any more. For the overwhelming majority of us, this is a simple, understandable, widely shared anxiety. While this anxiety is all but universal, thousands, maybe millions, of presentations are being made to large groups all over the country every day. Obviously, there are a lot of people out there managing the anxiety. You can, too.

Managing Anxiety: Preparation Phase

Managing anxiety is a two-step process. You must get control of it during the preparation phase, and then you must manage it during your actual persuasion (what we like to call "showtime"). To deal with your anxiety in the preparation phase, you should first remember James Garner. After all those seasons of beating up bad guys in front of the camera, he was afraid to make some remarks to a roomful of grateful and supportive people at the University of Oklahoma. You may be inclined to point out that he didn't really beat up those bad guys in front of the camera, and that's precisely the point. He's not a private detective, but he knows how to play one on television. And you don't have to be a confident speaker if you can play one on stage!

In the preparatory phase of your persuasion event, it's better not to try to overcome your anxiety. Instead, just reduce it so you can control it. In fact, some nervousness will be useful to you when you are in front of the audience. While you are preparing your remarks, concentrate on organizing your points and on reminding yourself that you have a starring role in a performance: you're the title character in a play called 'The Confident Speaker.'

Actors must master a myriad of postures, gestures, accents, and expressions in order to play major roles. As The Confident Speaker, however, you only have to master about a half dozen:

- stand up straight
- hold your head up
- keep your arms comfortably open at your sides unless you're gesturing
- gesture a lot, and do it expansively, with your whole arm
- project your voice to the back of the room
- make steady eye contact and look sincere.

Don't just plan on doing these things when you make your presentation. Rehearse them beforehand. Practice in front of a mirror, or make videos of yourself. Keep doing it until your body knows what it feels like to project your voice to the back of a room, to keep your shoulders back and your head up, to keep your hands at your sides unless you're gesturing. When you're gesturing, use your whole arm and gesture away from your body. If this sounds like work, it is. And that's part of the secret of reducing your anxiety. When you work, you burn off nervous and excess energy.

Also, when your body knows what it feels like to be this way, when you are actually relaxed with the posture and gestures of a confident speaker, you will be developing what we call "muscle memory." It is the exact same skill you use when you learn roller skating, saber fencing, high diving, or boxing. But nobody's going to punch you or thrust a sword at you, and you won't have to jump off a high diving board. Does that make the presentation seem a little less scary?

If you want to be a world-class persuader, you should start rehearsing now, whether you have a presentation coming up or not. Many people find the posture and gestures of the confident speaker unnatural. But the more you do them, the more natural they become.

Perhaps by telling you to learn to act like a confident speaker, we have converted your public speaking anxiety to stage fright. Not to worry. All actors suffer from stage fright. The best of them use it to provide the adrenalin needed to energize a performance. Yours will do the same, if you let it.

The trick to using your anxiety to energize (rather than debilitate) you is to know in advance you'll have anxiety and to know that much of it is caused by catastrophic thinking. When you think catastrophically, you don't let yourself contemplate actual consequences; you are simply overcome by a sort of nameless dread. When the dread is nameless, it is not a simple fear that's at work, but a fear of fear. Accepting the fear for what it is can help you avoid the fear of the fear, which is the cause of immobilizing panic. Step back from the dread and ask yourself what you're really afraid of. This helps you put a name to it, which is the first step of dealing with it. Are you afraid you'll die on the spot? Are you afraid the audience will rise up and throw things at you? Are such fears realistic, by any stretch of the imagination?

Maybe your fears are more modest. Maybe you're just worried about flubbing something or fainting. If so, take steps to prevent these things. If you're afraid of fainting, for example, slow your breathing (fainting from anxiety is caused by hyperventilating—stop the hyperventilation, and you remove the cause of the fainting). If you're afraid of your mind going blank, write some notes to keep in your pocket, so you can pull them out and consult them.

Above all, focus on the purpose of your presentation. Your attempt to persuade this audience is a valuable contribution to their lives. This is not about you, it's about them. Combine this understanding with whatever relaxation methods are effective for you (meditation, yoga, diaphragmatic breathing, relaxation exercises, and so on), and you will go a long way toward channeling your anxiety usefully.

Some speakers have little tricks for managing the symptoms of anxiety. One woman, who was worried about her mouth going dry (cotton mouth), figured out what makes her salivate. In her case, it was lemons. She found that whenever her mouth began to go dry, she could reactivate her salivary glands by calling up her mental picture of lemons.

Another speaker, who worried that his mind might go blank, habitually prepared himself with two file cards. On one he wrote an arresting fact or statistic about his subject, and on another he wrote the main points of his presentation. If his mind went blank, he pulled out his cards and said, "If I might digress for a moment, here's something interesting I would like to share with you." Then he would cite his arresting fact or statistic. If that did not unfreeze his memory, he went to the second card, and just picked a point and took the presentation from there. If he wound up skipping a point, it hardly mattered. The audience doesn't notice such things. In the end, the most memorable part of your presentation is you and the way you conduct yourself. That is what your audience will respond to.

Managing Anxiety: Presentation Phase

Anxiety about public speaking often stems from your beliefs about the audience. Perhaps this audience consists of strangers, which makes it easy for you to imagine they are hostile. Or maybe you know them, but you think they have reason to react with hostility. If the audience is truly hostile, it might not be exactly the right time to stage a persuasion event with them (although you may not have much choice). But it is important to separate the possibility of genuine hostility from your assumptions about it, which are nearly always rooted in fantasy and catastrophic thinking.

Make Friends

People who do a lot of public speaking agree that one of the best things you can do to control your anxiety at the presentation is to meet with members of the audience personally. Get there before the presentation and greet people as they arrive. Be friendly, and you will make friends with them. Even people who are actually hostile to your purpose will generally respond to an individual overture of friendliness.

If you've met audience members as individuals, you will not be confronting a faceless group. In fact, you'll be able to look to some of the friends you've made for encouragement. You can count on them to smile at you and nod.

Act the Part

Be sure to observe the posture, gestures, and expressions of the confident speaker (as described above). If you act confident, some part of your brain will believe you are confident, and you will burn off some of the nervous energy fueling your anxiety. The longer you act that way, the more surely you convince yourself. Breathe from your diaphragm, which will slow your breathing and keep you from hyperventilating. It will also slow your heartbeat and help you to relax.

Control your Brain

One tip for anxiety management you rarely see in the books and articles is gaze control. Don't scan the room with your eyes. As your presentation gets under way, address yourself to one person in the room at a time. Say a sentence or thought to one person, pause as you shift your gaze to another person, and then say another sentence. Keep doing it that way, one sentence or thought per person. This is actually good delivery technique because it helps to forge a bond between you and each audience member. But it's also a good self-control device. One of the biggest reasons for public speaking anxiety is the feeling of being overwhelmed that you get from scanning the audience. If you reduce the visual information overload by speaking to one person at a time, you eliminate the cause of that particular kind of anxiety. Control your eyes, in other words, and you control your brain.

Focus on the Topic

Focus your thinking on your presentation and the benefits you are offering the audience in being persuaded. This helps you to keep your mind off yourself. If you prevent your mind from thinking about yourself, you protect it from the fearing-the-fear stage.

Don't Share Nervousness

Finally, don't tell the audience that you feel nervous. It may feel to you like you're being candid and authentic, but making that particular complaint can sabotage you in two ways. In the first place, complaining about your nervousness reinforces it, as complaining always does. In the second place, your complaint takes some of the burden for your nervousness off you and puts it on the audience. They want you to succeed, and they identify with you up there. Telling them how uncomfortable you are is bound to affect their comfort level, and that lowers their receptivity to your message.

Nearly all books and articles that purport to advise you on overcoming anxiety about public speaking say very little about actually overcoming the anxiety. For the most part, they focus on the techniques of effective public speaking. This is a tacit recognition that in the end, there's no better cure for presentation anxiety than giving an outstanding presentation, so let's look at how that's done.

CHAPTER 4

Planning Your Presentation

PLAN YOUR PERSUASION EVENT AS YOU WOULD A MARKETING campaign. First, determine your goal. Second, analyze your market (the audience, in this case).

Know Your Goal

You probably have a good idea of your goal if you're going to attempt to persuade a large group. The whole point of persuasion, as we've defined it, is to change the attitude, belief, or point of view of another. But when you focus on your goal, you avoid the trap of thinking the presentation is an end in itself. And that is a trap, because it takes your mind off the audience. Persuasion is about them, not about you. You, after all, already hold the attitude, belief, or point of view at issue. Your goal is to get them to adopt it.

To keep your goal in front of you, you must first state it as simply and briefly as you can:

When my presentation is over, I want the audience to…

You would complete your goal sentence with a less active verb—understand, know, remember, and so forth—if you were planning an informational presentation. But this is a book about persuasion, and since you're reading it, you're probably not planning an informational presentation. You want to move your audience to action. That means completing the sentence with an active verb: adopt, reject, decide, move, change, reverse.

This table has some sample goal statements, designed to show the difference between those for an informational presentation and those for a persuasive presentation.

When my presentation is over, I want the audience to…

Informational presentation	Persuasive presentation
…understand my department's position on the new marketing plan.	…reject the new marketing plan.
…know how to read a quality analysis report.	…adopt the continuous quality improvement method.
…remember the importance of radio advertising in the marketing mix.	…change the marketing mix to give radio a 25% larger share.

Put your written statement of your goal somewhere you will see it while you're preparing your presentation. Compare every point you make to that goal. If the point doesn't seem to support the goal, reconsider it. When your goal is persuasion, a briefer presentation is nearly always better than a longer one.

Know Your Audience

The only way to persuade people is to show them the benefit of being persuaded. That means you need to understand what's in it for your audience to adopt the attitude, belief, or point of view that you want them to adopt. And to understand that, you first need to understand who they are.

Gather information on the audience. Start with the meeting-related stuff, move to the demographics, then go to the mind-set. In the Audience Analysis Worksheet, you can see the questions become more speculative toward the bottom.

Audience Analysis Worksheet

1. How many people will attend the meeting?
2. Why are they attending?
3. What is their relationship to the meeting?

4. Do they know each other?

5. What organization(s) do they come from?

6. What are their job functions?

7. What is their "rank" in relation to yours?

8. What is their general level of knowledge about the topic?

9. What is the range of their ages?

10. What is the gender mix?

11. What is the cultural diversity?

12. What is their primary language?

13. What do they have in common with you?

14. How do they feel about the position you want to persuade them to?

15. What are their aspirations?

16. What are their fears?

You probably don't have the time or resources to do a survey that might give you information about their aspirations and fears, but you can go a long way toward understanding a person's mind-set when you've gathered the answers to the questions higher up on the worksheet. It doesn't take a psychic to figure out, for example, that a group of management trainees aspire to have successful management careers, or that a group of CEOs fear a precipitous decline in the share prices of their companies.

This may be the toughest part of your preparations. You're trying to imagine the mind-set of other people. And imagining, as any novelist or screenwriter will tell you, is hard work.

Is It a Tough Room?

You can score the audience and calculate arithmetically how great a challenge you face in trying to persuade them. Use this test.

Scoring an Audience's Likely Responsiveness

A. How many people will attend your presentation?

1. 21 or more   **2.** 11-20   **3.** 6-10   **4.** 3-5

B. At the outset, what level of priority would this audience give your subject or topic?

1. Very high   **2.** High   **3.** Average   **4.** Low

C. How long is their attention span?

1. 20 minutes or more   **2.** 15 minutes   **3.** 10 minutes   **4.** 7 minutes or less

D. Do you know which audience members make or influence the decision?

1. Know exactly   **2.** Have a good idea   **3.** Have some idea   **4.** Not sure

E. How strong an impact will the benefits of your recommendation have?

1. Very strong   **2.** Better than average   **3.** Will put a dent in resistance
4. Will encounter strong opposition

Scoring

5-10   Easy Room. Use physical skills—volume, stance, and gestures—
to hold their attention and reinforce your credibility.

10-14   Challenging Room. Start by raising the priority level. Read your
audience one person at a time. Finish key ideas eye-to-eye with
decision-makers/influencers.

15-20   Tough Room. Pause. Control your nervousness with eye control.
Focus on benefits and supporting evidence.

What makes the toughest audience? A small group of children, likely to be resistant to your recommendation and with an uncertain ringleader. If you are a parent, you may recognize that situation! The second toughest audience is a small group of senior executives, opposed to your recommendation, in a state of distraction because of external events, and whose top decision-maker you can't identify. It is interesting that groups get tougher to persuade as they get smaller, but this may be because they are not amenable to showmanship. It is easier with a large group to incite enthusiasm because of the contagious nature of passion.

There is more about small groups in the section on persuading small groups.

What's In It for Your Audience?

In 1796, the government of France sent a 26-year-old general named Napoleon Bonaparte to assume the command of its army in Italy. The appointment was made for political reasons. Bonaparte's only military victory had taken place the year before when he gunned down several hundred civilians with grape shot on the steps of the Church of St. Roch in Paris.

He assumed command of an army that had stagnated at the foot of the Alps for three years. They were in poor physical condition, idle, underfed, and demoralized. Although he led them to success in a number of minor engagements shortly after his arrival, they had no real reason to put any faith in their 26-year-old general, much less conquer all of Italy for him.

But Napoleon knew the power of a persuasive speech:

Napoleon Takes Command

Soldiers, you have, in fifteen days, gained six victories, taken twenty-one stands of colors, fifty pieces of cannon, several fortified places, made fifteen hundred prisoners, and killed or wounded over ten thousand men. You are the equals of the conquerors of Holland and of the Rhine.

Destitute of everything, you have supplied yourselves with everything. You have won battles without cannon, crossed rivers without bridges, made forced marches without shoes, bivouacked without spirituous liquor, and often without bread. The Republican phalanxes—the soldiers of liberty, were alone capable of enduring what you have suffered.

Thanks to you, soldiers, your country has a right to expect of you great things. You have still battles to fight, cities to take, rivers to pass. Is there one among you whose courage flags? One who would prefer returning to the sterile summits of the Apennines and the Alps, to undergo patiently the insults of that slavish soldiery? No, there is not one such among the victors of Montenotte, of Millesimo, of Diego, and of Mondovi!

Friends, I promise you that glorious conquest: but be the liberators of peoples, be not their scourges!

Within a year, they had taken all of Italy and made Napoleon one of the most celebrated generals in history. Whenever his army entered an Italian city, they were celebrated and hailed as the deliverers of the populace.

Look at his speech. It has two characteristics that strike you immediately. First, it's short. It takes less than two minutes to read aloud, even with dramatic pauses. That's an important characteristic of persuasive speech—brevity. But the second characteristic is that the speech is less about Napoleon than it is about his audience. He compliments them on their achievements, sympathizes with them over their hardships, and promises them glory. The word "I" only appears once, and even then, it's about what he intends to do for them.

For an interesting contrast, look at the speech made by the same man 20 years later, after he'd been Emperor of the French and the most powerful man in Europe for over a decade. Here is Napoleon's 1814 speech abdicating his throne:

Napoleon Abdicates

Soldiers, I bid you farewell. For twenty years that we have been together your conduct has left me nothing to desire. I have always found you on the road to glory. All the powers of Europe have combined in arms against me.

A few of my generals have proved untrue to their duty and to France. France herself has desired other destinies; with you and the brave men who still are faithful, I might have carried on a civil war; but France would be unhappy. Be faithful, then, to your new king, be obedient to your new commanders, and desert not our beloved country.

Do not lament my lot; I will be happy when I know that you are so. I might have died; if I consent to live, it is still to promote your glory. I will write the great things that we have achieved.

I cannot embrace you all, but I embrace your general. Come, General Petit, that I may press you to my heart! Bring me the eagle, that I may embrace it also! Ah! dear eagle, may this kiss which I give thee find an echo to the latest posterity! Adieu, my children; the best wishes of my heart shall be always with you: do not forget me!

This one is all about Napoleon. It may have brought tears to the eyes of some of his veterans, but it is not persuasive. Its only attempt at persuasion ("Be faithful, then, to your new king, be obedient to your new commanders") was obviously a failure, because he was back the next year, and the army deserted its new king and commanders to fight for him at Waterloo!

It is clear, however, that at the beginning of his career, Napoleon had an extraordinary sense of his audience and was prepared to offer its members a major benefit for supporting him.

The audience analysis you have just performed is what you will use to determine what benefits you can offer the audience for adopting the point of view you want them to adopt. You may not be in the position to offer them military glory. But you must ask yourself how their lives are going to be improved by adopting the position or point of view you want them to adopt. Hint: it probably has little or nothing to do with your happiness or well-being.

There may be a dozen benefits for an audience to adopt the point of view you want them to adopt, but there is one benefit (or at most two) that is dominant. Note that the dominant benefit may vary from audience to audience. For example, if your persuasion event is intended to get an audience of consumers to buy a particular breakfast cereal, the dominant benefits would be different for kids and their parents. You might persuade an audience of kids to eat it because it tastes good or because of its radioactive color. But you would persuade an audience of parents to buy it for their kids because it's easy to get them to eat it.

The dominant benefit is the basis of your benefit statement. The benefit statement is a single-sentence statement of what your presentation is about. Imagine yourself standing at the doorway to the hall where you will be giving your presentation, and a member of the audience comes up and asks you if the session will be worth his time. You will tell him that it is indeed worth his time. Then he asks you what it's about. Your benefit statement is the one-sentence answer to that question. "This presentation is about how your department will gain prestige and security by adopting continuous quality improvement." Or, "This presentation is about how your sales will improve by increasing the share of radio advertising to 25% in your marketing plan." Or, "This presentation will give you a glimpse of the glory and immortality we can achieve by conquering Italy in the name of the Republic."

Once you've formulated your benefit statement, use it to shape your presentation. In a very real sense, it's the whole point of what you're saying. And memorize it, so you'll have it ready in case any members of your audience ask you beforehand whether they should attend. You'd be surprised how often that happens!

CHAPTER 5

The Format for Persuasion

SO FAR, YOU'VE DONE NOTHING ON THE ACTUAL PRESENTATION, which is where most business professionals start on this process. Here's the way most people do it (or, as we like to say, the wrong way):

1. Go to the computer and launch Microsoft Office.
2. Click on the "AutoContent Wizard" button with the PowerPoint icon on it.
3. Choose a type of presentation from the list provided.
4. Substitute text in the bullet-point outline provided by the AutoContent Wizard.
5. Add clip art, cartoons, and charts.
6. Save file.
7. Send file to meeting organizer so somebody can write a press release about the forthcoming presentation.

The AutoContent Wizard has templates for at least 20 different kinds of presentations, including "Managing Organizational Change," "Motivating a Team," "Recommending a Strategy," and "Communicating Bad News." The templates are based on tested formulas for successful presentations. As a result, the AutoContent Wizard in PowerPoint knows how to make a presentation that is about 90% of what any business professional needs to accomplish in a presentation. Most people are pleased with a grade of 80%. No wonder PowerPoint is so popular!

While the AutoContent Wizard's outlines are highly serviceable and can almost guarantee you a set of slides that will look professional, it will not achieve persuasion for you. All it can do is help you stay neat, organized, and reasonably well designed. PowerPoint, in other words, can help to keep you from looking bad. That's no mean achievement for a piece of software. But it's not persuasion.

In fact, it's safe to say that a spectacular set of slides—with fancy transitions, animations, informative charts, and beautifully chosen colors—will be more of an obstacle than an enhancement to your persuasion efforts. Why? Spectacular slides focus the audience's attention away from you. And you are the single most important variable in the persuasion equation. Persuasion is a transaction between each person in the audience and you. Whether or not it happens depends on your confidence, your passion, your sincerity, and how much the audience trusts you. The most beautiful slides in the world can add nothing to those qualities. They can never do more than clarify what you are saying to the audience or occasionally entertain it.

If you've been told to give a presentation, PowerPoint may help you do it at least as well as most business professionals do it. But if you need to achieve persuasion, you must spend more time preparing yourself than you spend preparing your slides. By all means, create a PowerPoint file for your persuasive presentation. But understand that it is only one of the steps in your preparation.

Writing Out the Presentation

There's a perennial question about preparing a presentation. Should you write it out? We advise you to do so if writing it out builds your confidence and makes you feel comfortable about giving the presentation.

Having written it out, you should read it over. Then read it over again. Then read it aloud. Then use it to rehearse the posture and gestures of the Confident Speaker. Then read it to yourself in a mirror, but be sure to look at yourself at least as much as you look at your manuscript.

Then make an outline of it. Study the outline and try delivering the speech from just the outline. Then reduce the outline to its major points, and try delivering the presentation from those alone.

In short, we think you should read your written presentation to yourself, your family, your friends, and your pets. You should use it as a script for your rehearsals. Just don't try to read it to the audience. The audience doesn't care how well you read aloud. They want to connect with you as a person. Whether or not you wrote the presentation yourself doesn't matter, although you can be sure they will doubt you did write it if you stand in front of them and read it. As long as you're reading to the audience, you're not giving them a "live" presentation. You are a playback machine for a manuscript. You will not persuade them of anything.

If, on the other hand, writing out your remarks ahead of time helps you to prepare to deliver them as a person rather than a playback machine, writing out the presentation is a great idea.

The Format for Persuasion

We recommend one format for persuading a large group. It has five parts:

- Opener
- Recommendation
- Benefits
- Support
- Action

This is not the only possible format for a persuasive argument, but we recommend it because it keeps you focused on the audience rather than your recommendation. Let's look at each element of the format.

Opener

The opener has a single purpose: to make the audience feel a pain that can only be relieved by adopting your recommendation. If you think there isn't any pain that can be relieved by adopting your recommendation, then either the time is not right to be persuading this audience, or you aren't being sufficiently imaginative in what you define as pain. You cannot persuade them unless you offer them a benefit, and that benefit is invariably a relief of their pain.

There are three kinds of pain your recommendation might relieve:
- problem (an obstacle that stands between your audience and achievement of a goal)
- opportunity (a chance for an advantage in achieving a goal)
- weakness (a deficiency that undermines your audience's effectiveness in striving toward a goal).

The middle one, opportunity, might not seem very painful at first glance, but the key here is the cost of forgone opportunity. Imagine, for example, the cell phone manufacturer who several years ago said, "What's the point of putting a camera into a phone?" Missing an opportunity that is then taken by someone else is one of the deepest, most enduring types of pain to be found in business.

So, whether you're selling a software product, soliciting contributions to conquer a disease, trying to reorganize a company division, proposing the development of a new product, or taking a company in a new direction, your recommendation is a cure for one of these three types of pain.

Look at the three types of pain again: problem, opportunity, weakness. You'll never forget what they are if you arrange them into an acronym—Problem, Opportunity, Weakness—that spells POW!

The POW! opener gets the audience's attention and lets them know they are in pain. The idea is not to dwell on the pain. When people don't know they are in pain, it can be difficult to help them see it. So this step has to be done carefully. First, compose a single sentence that describes and quantifies:
- "Interdepartmental communication problems delayed our last product rollout by six weeks."
- "If we miss the opportunity to put cameras in our cell phones, we will lose a market worth $3 million annually."
- "Our inability to secure reliable shipping has cost us our two largest accounts, which were responsible for $250,000 in revenue annually."

This sentence is not part of your presentation. It is the basis for the brief story you are going to tell that humanizes the pain:

- "I was at an electronics show recently, and I saw a strange product. Someone had taken a cell phone like the one we manufacture and had added a CCD chip to it so it could take digital pictures. And I had a vision of a girl calling her friend and saying, 'I'm at the mall. What do you think of these jeans?' or a motorist reporting an accident to the police saying, 'It looks like somebody might be hurt.' And I realized the added dimension of sending a photo on a phone call is what the world has been waiting for."

- "I had a talk with our biggest account today, and she said she's taking her business to our principal competitor because we can't guarantee reliable shipping."

- "I went to the discount electronics store, and I walked up to the shelf where our new product was supposed to be, and I saw a generous supply of our competitors' product. The clerk came up and offered to help me, and he demonstrated our competitors' product for me, insisting it was the latest thing. I tried to tell him there was another, even better, product on the way, and he just looked at me like I'd come from Mars, as if to say, 'What could be better than the one I have in my hand?'"

Recommendation

You have the audience's attention now, and they understand there's a problem, opportunity, or weakness. If you have humanized it with a story, they very likely agree with your assessment of the situation. Now it's time, while the pain is uppermost in their minds, to tell them how to relieve it. State your recommendation.

Your recommendation is not some generalized thing like, "Let's all pull together." People dismiss such platitudes out of hand. Your recommendation must be specific, and it must tell the people in the audience what to do. This is not the time to get into details. At this stage of your presentation, your recommendation is a vision of the future. Create that vision as simply as possible:

- "We must start making camera phones in time to have them on the shelves before the next buying season."

- "We're going to require a performance guarantee from any shipping vendor that does business with us, and we're going to put a monitoring system in place to measure performance."

- "My recommendation is to tie performance evaluations and bonuses in these two departments to their success in meeting deadlines on the next product rollout."

Benefits

Up to this point, we've gotten the audience's attention by showing them they are in pain, and given them a glimpse of how to relieve that pain. Now it's time to walk them over the bridge to the informational part of the presentation. That bridge is the benefit of adopting your recommendation.

In a way, every persuasion event is a sales transaction. The audience must always give up something (even if it is only a point of view with which they are comfortable) in order to adopt your recommendation. Whatever it is the audience must give up can be viewed as the purchase price of your recommendation. This is what salespeople deal with all the time. They show customers the benefits of whatever it is they are selling so the customers can decide whether the thing is worth the purchase price.

To show your audience your recommendation is worth it, you explain the benefits—how the recommendation will make their lives better.

These benefits are specific, and they specifically apply to members of the audience. Remember, we are talking about a particular impact on their lives. Will it:

- Let them get their work done quicker?
- Make their jobs more secure?
- Make their vacations longer?
- Make them more prestigious or powerful?
- Make their neighborhoods safer?
- Let their kids get better grades?

Figure out two benefits to the audience of your recommendation. State the strongest benefit second, where it will be more prominent. The description of a benefit, incidentally, nearly always includes some form of the word "you."

When you state a benefit, imagine a specific, quantifiable outcome you can use to make it real. Don't say, "This will let you get your work done quicker." Say, "This will let you go home at 4:00 each day." Don't say, "This will make your neighborhood safer." Say, "This will let you walk around the neighborhood in the evening again."

In other words, create a mental picture for them of what their lives will be like after adopting your recommendation.

Support

At this point, the audience should be sympathetic to your recommendation. Many of them want to adopt it. After all, they have pain, they have glimpsed the cure for that pain, and now they have seen the benefit to their life of adopting it. Now you deal with whatever remaining skepticism they might have by offering evidence to support your recommendation.

Evidence for a persuasion event comes in five forms:
- data
- expertise
- cases
- image
- story

The first, data, is the one used most often in presentations. Data are the statistics and facts that have put so many of us to sleep in the course of someone else's presentation. You need to remember that data is one type of evidence among many, and it's not the most effective type. Pull it all together, then choose a few of your most powerful data points to present. Keep the rest for the question-and-answer period.

The second type of evidence, expertise, is the opinion of someone your audience will accept as an authority on the subject—an expert, in other words. Expert opinion is valuable if you have it. That's one of the reasons they use it in court during trials.

The third type of evidence, cases, is most useful when you have examples that are close to the experience of your audience members or particularly meaningful to them. Cases or examples are particularly useful because they show real world applications.

The fourth type of evidence, image, is used by way of analogy to relate this new thing (your recommendation) to something familiar. Image is an explanatory form of evidence; it doesn't prove anything. To say that your new centralized production plan operates like the solar system, with Department X in the center, is just a way to help the audience visualize it. Analogies are only suggestive.

The fifth type of evidence, story, is something from your personal experience. It may not readily prove your contentions, but it brings them to life.

The five types of evidence—Data, Expertise, Cases, Image, Story—help your audience come to a decision about your recommendation, and they form an acronym: decision.

Evidence will probably be the largest single section of your presentation. You can be a little more expansive with it than you are with the other sections. But don't make the mistake of many speakers, who think they will do well to overwhelm the audience with evidence and wear down their resistance. You may indeed be able to wear them down, but bored people are not persuaded. They're just bored.

Action

The last step before questions and answers is to ask the audience to take the first step toward implementing your recommendation. This prevents them from putting off the decision, and it involves them in its implementation. In order to make sure they act, you must assign a deadline. All presentations include this action step, and it's often something like, "We need to contact the following shippers by Tuesday and ask them if they are willing to give us performance guarantees in return for a specified amount of business."

But a persuasion event requires a certain kind of action step, and it always has the same deadline: "Before we leave here today…"

You must devise some substantive step that can be taken immediately. This gains your audience's commitment to the recommendation, and it gives the plan a constituency: people who have already invested some effort in it:

"Before we leave here today, we must designate a committee to set objectives for interdepartmental communication and review the bonus structure."

CHAPTER **6**

Making Visuals

MOST BUSINESS PRESENTATIONS MAKE HEAVY USE OF VISUALS. As we noted in the Principles of Persuasion (number five), visuals let you approach your audience through more than one channel of communication. They also clarify concepts that might be unclear when simply stated in words.

Most business professionals, in fact, seem to believe that creating a set of slides is the same thing as creating a presentation. Then they stand in front of the audience as the slides appear and use the slides as a script. This is a terrible thing to do to an audience, whether you're trying to persuade them or not.

If you've done the background research for your persuasion event, you probably have a mountain of data, charts, illustrations, bulleted lists, and graphics. And you are no doubt tempted to use all of it in your slides. But the audience isn't interested in how much information you have managed to dig up. They are interested in the position you propose to move them to and why you think they should adopt it. Your visuals can never tell your story. Only you can tell your story.

Try this as an experiment. Get your Walkman or your iPod or whatever you use for listening to music and cue up some music that you're fond of, preferably something with meaningful lyrics. Put on the headphones and start listening to the music. Now pick up this book and resume reading.

Are you reading this with someone singing in your ears? Are you getting 100% of the meaning from each? No? Maybe you should stop listening until you're done reading. We'll wait if you want to listen to the rest of the current song.

What you've just been through is what happens to the audience when you put a highly detailed visual up on the screen during your presentation. You know the kind we're talking about: a table with four or six columns and 15 or 20 rows, which yields at least 60 data points, plus another 20 or so column and row headings. When you put something like that up on the screen, the audience immediately starts reading, to try to make sense out of it. Meanwhile, you're talking, but they're studying the column headings, examining numbers, and looking for trends. Their ability to comprehend what you're saying is compromised.

Most of the rules for creating effective visuals are variations on keeping them simple. Let's look at the 10 most important of these.

1. Read Horizontally

Make sure all the "action" in your visuals goes horizontally from left to right. This goes without saying for text, but make sure your charts, graphs, tables, and images work that way as well. Audiences in the business world are thoroughly conditioned to left-to-right reading. Any attempt to get them to follow a story up, down, or right-to-left is going to cost them effort, which is a distraction from what you are saying.

2. Use Upper and Lower Case

Study after study of legibility has shown that people read upper and lower case text more readily than they read capitalized text. There's a lot of theory to explain this, but you can prove it to yourself by comparing two lines of text: one upper and lower case, one all caps. And for titles, you should use initial capital letters. It's a widely accepted convention, and it's also more readable than either all uppercase or all lowercase.

3. Highlight Key Words

When you have text on the screen, it will help your audience a great deal if you do something to make key words stand out. There are a lot of highlighting possibilities: font change, different typeface, underline, size change, color change. Of all these possibilities, font change (i.e., bold rather than regular) and color change are the best, either alone or in combination. Both are instantly recognizable and tend to create the least disruption in the design of the screen.

4. Use Two to Four Colors for Text

Using the same color of text throughout can be boring, and boredom lowers alertness levels. But using too many colors can overwhelm the audience. Two colors per screen is very effective. If you need a third and fourth color for headers, headlines, or special emphasis, that's fine.

5. Bullets: the Rule of Four

Never use more than four bullet points per screen and never more than four words per bullet. Anything more can dramatically reduce the audience's comprehension and increase the strain of trying to understand the points. The one exception is the technique of "building" the bullets. When you have a single screen that adds the bullets as you present them, you can use more than four, because people are never trying to take in more than one at a time.

6. Check Spelling

Misspelled words don't make you look defiant of conventions or rebellious. They just make you look sloppy. The law of averages dictates that every audience includes at least one person who is a skilled speller. And if there's an Iron Law of Persuasion, it's that no skilled speller was ever persuaded by visuals with misspellings.

7. Use Pictures

Photos, clip art, or cartoons can make points that would take forever to get across with words, and they can do it more dramatically. They are especially useful for the type of evidence we described above as "image."

8. One Graph Per Slide

Graphs can be a great way to show trends, relationships, and proportions. But putting more than one on a slide increases the effort required by your audience to interpret.

9. Minimize Special Effects

Animations and fancy transitions can be effective when they are used sparingly. But more than one special effect per presentation may be too many. As we have noted, special effects take the focus away from you.

10. Save Details for Handouts

One way to provide the audience with some of that mountain of information you have assembled is to put it in handouts to distribute after your remarks. They can study the details later.

7

Persuasion Showtime

AFTER YOU'VE ORGANIZED YOUR PRESENTATION AND REHEARSED it extensively, you will present it. This chapter explains in more detail how to play the role of the Confident Speaker, because that confidence is responsible for a major share of your persuasive effect on the audience. In chapter three, we explained how to control your anxiety while you were preparing your presentation. In this chapter, we will share ways to control it when you're in front of an audience.

Stance

You will appear most in control in front of an audience if you stand with your feet hip-width apart and distribute your weight equally between them. Don't pace. Don't shift your weight from foot to foot. You may find it difficult to avoid shifting around or making little nervous gestures. But you must train yourself in the posture of the Confident Speaker. Any other posture or movement distracts the audience from your message.

The posture of the Confident Speaker is actually a form of camouflage. It is the least distracting appearance you can offer on a stage. And because the audience detects so few distractions, you can force them to focus on your facial expression and your hand gestures, both of which reinforce your message.

Gestures

Don't put your hands in your pockets. Don't clasp your hands in front of you. Keep your hands at your sides unless you are gesturing, and gesture frequently to emphasize and "illustrate" points. Gestures make you the center of the action and continually refocus the audience's attention on you.

Gestures should be expansive. Make gestures with your whole arm, above the waist, and away from your body. Gesture with one arm at a time. Two-arm gestures tend to get your hands working together, and that can be distracting to the audience. Match the gestures to what you are saying. If you want to say the trend on a graph is upward, sweep upward with your arm. If you want to say costs have to be cut, cut the air with your arm.

Eye Control

We have already mentioned eye control in the section on managing anxiety. Eye control does help to manage anxiety, but it also enhances your presence as a speaker. It increases the comfort level of the audience, and it increases their connection to you.

Again, eye control consists of limiting your gaze. As you speak, look into the eyes of an audience member. Continue to look into that person's eyes until you have completed a thought or a sentence, pause, then move your gaze to another person's eyes. In addition to strengthening the audience's connection with you, it also has the advantage of giving you the opportunity to see how the audience is reacting to you. It also allows you to get support from smiles and nods of encouragement, which you cannot see when you scan the audience or watch your visuals.

Eye control means focusing on one person at a time. It has at least three benefits:
- reduces anxiety
- helps you think on your feet
- gives you a chance to read your audience.

Voice

Project your voice to the person in the back of the room and speak forcefully. If you are using a microphone, you should still project your voice and speak forcefully. Speaking forcefully will give your voice passion. A microphone amplifies that passion. Don't worry about being too loud. You cannot be too loud without a microphone, and if you do have one, you can always turn the volume down, but don't turn it down more than you need to keep from breaking the windows with your voice.

Most presenters speak at the mid-point of the volume they are capable of, i.e., on a scale of 1 to 10, they speak at 5. But at volume 7 or 8, audiences recognize the speaker as being authoritative. So speak at 7 or 8 and get that extra benefit.

Avoid using nonwords like "um." Analyze your voice on tape to know what yours are and when you tend to use them, then control them.

Vary the tone and pitch of your voice. Match its expression to the things you are saying, of course. But don't let yourself slip into that seductive monologue that you may think makes you sound "businesslike." This is a performance.

Passion

Don't act passionate about your recommendation; be passionate about it. If you feel deeply about the position or point of view you're trying to persuade the audience to, let that feeling come out. The audience will perceive it and be moved. Passion is communicable. If you don't feel deeply about your recommendation, why are you trying to persuade anyone to adopt it?

Work with your Visuals

Remember that as soon as you put a new slide up on the screen, it's news and it takes the audience's attention off you. Get their attention back quickly and efficiently by "clearing the news." Tell them what is on slide. If it is a set of bullet points, for example, go through them before discussing any of them in detail. Make sure you are facing the audience when you give them the points. Look at the slide (which directs the audience attention to it), read the bullet point silently, then turn to the audience (which brings their attention back to you), and say the point. Do this bullet by bullet. We call it "think-turn-talk."

Look for the Bell Cow

Remember, the persuasion event is about the audience. It's not about you. Your primary concern is whether they are moving toward the position you want them to take. You are watching them one person at a time while you are presenting. Look for signs of approval or disapproval.

Think about the last time you attended a presentation in which the speaker said at one point, "I see some of you are shaking your heads." Didn't that raise your interest level? It always does, because it is a sign the speaker is interacting with the audience. A persuasion event is always a conversation. The audience doesn't usually speak during your presentation, but they are still having the conversation. They are making their points with expressions and posture. Watch for what they say.

Marketers talk about something called the "bell cow" phenomenon. Bell cows are opinion leaders, and they can be found in any group. When you're persuading a large group, the bell cow may be the most senior person in the room, but not always. In any case, if you have been able to identify the bell cow, then that's the person you should be most interested in watching, because when that person makes up her mind, much of the rest of the group is likely to follow. In some cases, the persuasion may even come down to a conversation between you and the bell cow, with the rest of the audience acting as spectators.

Question and Answer

If you have a question-and-answer session that is long and animated, it is the best sign you could hope for that you are achieving persuasion. You should allow as much time as you can for questions. In the standard one-hour session, most speakers allocate 45 minutes for themselves and 15 minutes for questions. The most confident and successful speakers use the reverse of that ratio. Remember, it's about the audience, not you!

Think about it. If you are able to get the audience truly excited about your idea, they will want to spend as much time as possible learning more about it and contributing their insights to it. For this reason, skilled persuaders know that the question-and-answer period is even more important than the formal presentation, and they spend most of their time preparing for it.

To anticipate questions so you can prepare for them, look at your presentation from the audience's point of view. Again, we are back to the question with which we began this chapter: what's in it for them?

Think about whom your recommendation could hurt and whom it could disproportionately benefit. You will surely get follow-up questions in each of those areas. Think about your qualifications to present this recommendation. Think about what you've done to lead up to this, and think about how you benefit from the recommendation. Then think about all the technical points of the evidence that may not be abundantly or immediately clear. Write out in advance whatever questions you can anticipate, and develop the phrasings you will use to answer.

Take Control

After you have concluded the formal part of your remarks and you're ready for questions, show the audience how to ask them. Raise your hand and ask if they have questions. When they see your hand raised, they will know they need to be recognized before asking anything. This keeps things orderly, and it helps audience members avoid embarrassment by talking over each other. It also gives the more reticent members of the audience a chance to ask their questions.

Maintain your Confident Speaker posture as you stand there with your hand raised. Extend your other hand toward the audience in a welcoming gesture. It will ordinarily take about 15 seconds for someone to formulate and ask a question. Fill the gap with friendly-sounding remarks, like, "I've been looking forward to hearing from you on this topic. Please ask whatever questions you have, and I'll answer them if I can."

When someone raises a hand, acknowledge it by saying, "I see one question over there, and I will take that one first. Are there any others?" As other hands pop up, recognize them by saying, "Yes, here's another... and another..." and so on. Then go back to the first hand that was raised, extend your hand with an open palm toward the person, and say, "We'll start with the first person who raised her hand. What is your question, please?"

Information Questions

There are two kinds of questions that will be raised: information questions and audience pressure questions. Information questions are easiest to deal with, at least emotionally, but don't think that means they don't require effort.

Most people running a question-and-answer session begin thinking about how they are going answer as soon as the questioner begins the question. Bad idea. Listen to the question. In fact, listen to more than the question. Listen for the issue the question represents. It will probably fall into one of five areas:

- priority/importance
- feasibility
- cost
- timing
- competence/quality

When the questioner has finished stating the question, rephrase the question to someone else in the audience.

Rephrasing the question has a benefit for the audience: it allows everyone in the room to hear the question.

But rephrasing has even more advantages for you. First of all, it gives you time to think about your answer.

A second, and more subtle, benefit for you is that rephrasing the question makes the question-and-answer session more interactive and less transactional. It puts you and the audience into a more cooperative relationship as you work out together what the question means. This increases audience sympathy for you.

But the third benefit of rephrasing the question is probably the most important: it maintains your control over the process. In the time you are rephrasing, you can be formulating and refining your answer, and that interval is often a blessing. But this act also makes you the focus of the exchange.

Rephrase simple, informational questions in terms similar to those used by the questioner:

Question: How do you propose to market camera phones?
Rephrase: How will we market camera phones?

As questions get more complex, rephrasing—coupled with your listening for the issue—can make them manageable:

Question: On what basis would you prioritize the failure of interdepartmental communication as the cause of our product rollout delay?

Rephrase: How do we know the failure of interdepartmental communication caused the delay in our product rollout?

Audience Pressure

Up until now we have been talking about informational questions, but we all know there is a second variety of question that comes up during presentations: the hostile or challenging question we call the audience pressure question.

Deal with a challenging question by first listening for the issue. You must respond to the issue rather than the challenge or the hostility. Perhaps the most common challenge question is "Why are you proposing this?"

Depending on which words of the question are emphasized by the questioner, this could be aimed at any of the five common issues. It could be a question of priority (i.e., "Why are you proposing this and not something else?"), feasibility (i.e., "How can we hope to accomplish this?"), cost ("Why should we spend money on this?"), timing ("Why should we do this now?"), or competence ("Who are you to propose this?").

You may have to listen carefully to get a sense of which area the questioner is addressing. But if you rephrase by naming the issue, you can make the question neutral:

Question: Why are you proposing this?
Rephrase: Are we competent to implement this recommendation?

Explain, neutrally and briefly, why you are competent to implement the recommendation, and conclude the answer on a positive note, like, "We've never been better prepared for a program like this."

Your answer needs one more thing. Tie it to the benefits you cited during the formal part of the presentation: "That's how I think it will save us millions of dollars."

By rephrasing on the issue and responding to the issue in a positive way and then relating the answer to the benefits, you can neutralize almost any challenging or hostile question and reinforce your persuasive message. Above all, don't ever lose your temper. Remember the audience is evaluating you, and anything that makes them uncomfortable raises their resistance to being persuaded.

PART III
Persuading Small Groups

CHAPTER **8**

Analyzing a Small Audience

WE DEFINE A SMALL GROUP AS ONE TO FOUR PEOPLE. The lower end of that range—one person—may not seem like a group at all, and it isn't. But, other things being equal, there is no substantive difference between trying to persuade one-on-one and trying to persuade one-on-two, or one-on-three, or one-on-four.

But there are many ways in which trying to persuade a small group is different from trying to persuade a large group. For one thing, you are usually sitting down when you try to persuade a small group, so your presentation style will be fundamentally different. But you also prepare for a small group persuasion differently than you prepare for the persuasion of a large audience.

Your Audience

You probably won't have stage fright or public speaking anxiety if you're going to give a presentation to a small group. The numbers simply aren't as intimidating. But you may have anxiety for other reasons. The people in a small group are more likely to be higher-level decision makers than the people in a large group, and you will often have more at stake in a small group persuasion than a large-group persuasion. Some of the anxiety management techniques you read about in chapter five may be useful, but the best thing you can do is to focus on your goal. What do you want these people to do as a result of your presentation? You might even try visualizing them doing it.

If you read the chapter on persuading a large group, you will remember that your goal statement—the description of what you want the audience to do—uses a less active verb like understand, know, or remember when your presentation is informational. But you state the goal for a persuasive presentation with an active verb such as adopt, reject, decide, move, change, or reverse.

This table, reproduced from chapter four, has some sample goal statements, designed to show the difference between those for an informational presentation and those for a persuasive presentation.

When my presentation is over, I want the audience to…

Informational presentation	Persuasive presentation
…understand my department's position on the new marketing plan.	…reject the new marketing plan.
…know how to read a quality analysis report.	…adopt the continuous quality improvement method.
…remember the importance of radio advertising in the marketing mix.	…change the marketing mix to give radio a 25% larger share.

Put your written statement of your goal somewhere you will see it while you're preparing your presentation. Compare every point you make to that goal. If the point doesn't seem to support the goal, reconsider it. When your goal is persuasion, a briefer presentation is nearly always better than a longer one.

Audience Analysis for a Small Group

If you read the section on large group persuasion, you may remember this worksheet on audience scoring.

Scoring an Audience's Likely Responsiveness

A. How many people will attend your presentation?

1. 21 or more   **2.** 11-20   **3.** 6-10   **4.** 3-5

B. At the outset, what level of priority would this audience give your subject or topic?

1. Very high   **2.** High   **3.** Average   **4.** Low

C. How long is their attention span?

1. 20 minutes or more   **3.** 10 minutes

2. 15 minutes   **4.** 7 minutes or less

D. Do you know which audience members make or influence the decision?

1. Know exactly   **3.** Have some idea

2. Have a good idea   **4.** Not sure

E. How strong an impact will the benefits of your recommendation have?

1. Very strong   **3.** Will put a dent in resistance

2. Better than average   **4.** Will encounter strong opposition

Scoring

5-10   Easy Room. Use physical skills—volume, stance, and gestures—to hold their attention and reinforce your credibility.

10-14   Challenging Room. Start by raising the priority level. Read your audience one person at a time. Finish key ideas eye-to-eye with decision-makers/influencers.

15-20   Tough Room. Pause. Control your nervousness with eye control. Focus on benefits and supporting evidence.

The bad news about small groups is that the room gets tougher as the audience grows smaller. We pointed out in chapter six that it was because the contagious nature of passion makes it easier (other things being equal) to incite enthusiasm in a large group. But there's another factor at work here: smaller groups are nearly always composed of more high-powered individuals. When you are trying to persuade fewer than five people it usually means you are trying to persuade the leadership of an organization, and leaders tend to be more skeptical. That's part of what they are paid to be.

The good news about small groups is that it's possible to learn more about them. First, complete an audience analysis worksheet.

Audience Analysis Worksheet

1. How many people will attend the meeting?
2. Why are they attending?
3. What is their relationship to the meeting?

4. Do they know each other?

5. What organization(s) do they come from?

6. What are their job functions?

7. What is their "rank" in relation to yours?

8. What is their general level of knowledge about the topic?

9. What is the range of their ages?

10. What is the gender mix?

11. What is the cultural diversity?

12. What is their primary language?

13. What do they have in common with you?

14. How do they feel about the position you want to persuade them to?

15. What are their aspirations?

16. What are their fears?

For a small group, however, that worksheet is only the beginning. For a small group, you ought to be able to compile a profile of each person with whom you will be meeting.

Your sources of information for the profiles are colleagues, friends, and co-workers. These can give you information about job description, tenure, history, and interests. But don't neglect nontraditional sources. It is often surprising how much you can find out about someone just by doing a web search on her name. Web searches turn up magazine interviews, publications, and sometimes biographies prepared by a company's public relations department.

Ideally, you want to understand something about each person's hopes, fears, aspirations, goals, drivers—whatever you can learn that will give you some insight into how this person makes decisions.

You will need some structure for your investigation, some question you can ask about a person's fundamental drivers that will direct your understanding. There are literally hundreds of psychological profiling theories: introvert/extrovert, Jungian types, Type A/Type B, Theory X/Theory Y, "emotional intelligence," visual-aural-kinesthetic perception, various personality scales... the list is endless. None of these is more correct than any of the others. Each is just a structured way of looking at people, and that's what you want to use when you compile your profiles of individual audience members.

If you don't have a favorite among all these psychological theories, here's an informal one you may find useful. In most decisions faced by a human being, one alternative offers change and the other alternative offers stability. People tend to choose one or the other most of the time. That is, some people choose the adventure and the novelty of change, while some choose the predictability and comfort of stability. This isn't a value judgment about people, and it doesn't mean that people always choose one way or the other. But knowing which way a person tends to choose on that question gives you some insight into how you can best frame your proposal.

To a change seeker, you will want to emphasize the way your proposal breaks with tradition or the way it innovates, or how it is in line with the latest thinking on a certain subject. To a stability seeker, you will want to emphasize how your proposal helps to protect assets, capitalizes on existing skills and talents, or fits in with an organization's original mission.

So, as you research your audience members, ask yourself whether each person's history indicates a preference for change or stability. But be careful. History is not always indicative of the current situation. Prepare arguments for both approaches and be prepared to switch if you discover in the meeting that somebody isn't just what you thought he was.

And of course you must ask the most important question about your proposal: what's in it for the audience?

CHAPTER

9

Structuring a Presentation for a Small Group

MANY PEOPLE FEEL THAT A SMALL GROUP PERSUASION EVENT requires a different kind of presentation than a large group event. A small group persuasion is different from a large group presentation, but it requires just as much structure and just as much rehearsal.

In chapter five, we discussed whether it makes sense to write out your presentation for a large group. Many people wouldn't even ask that question about a small group presentation, because they assume it will be more like a conversation than a presentation. In fact, you should run it like a conversation. But you should prepare for it like a presentation.

The same advice applies. Write out your presentation if it makes you feel comfortable to do so. Take your written version and rehearse with it. Present it to friendly audiences such as close friends, spouses, or pets. Use the written version as source material for an outline or for notes. Never bring the written version with you to the presentation.

Small group persuasion uses the same five-step format we presented for large-group persuasion:

- Opener
- Recommendation
- Benefits
- Support
- Action

Use the Psychological Profiles

When you do your research on the audience, one of the members will no doubt be the major decision maker, the bell cow. You will probably need to persuade all of them, but it's in the nature of small groups that they tend to follow the bell cow, even more so than large groups. In a small group, there is less "cover" for the followers. Even if they don't follow the bell cow, they are likely to be easier to persuade once you win the bell cow over. So spend the lion's share of your preparation effort addressing the needs and concerns of the bell cow.

Opener

As with a large-group persuasion, the opener has a single purpose: to make the audience feel a pain that can only be relieved by adopting your recommendation. But for a small group persuasion, you will be working from the deeper audience analysis you conducted. Remember, your recommendation is a cure for a problem or a weakness or a way to seize an opportunity. So your opener focuses on a problem, opportunity, or weakness—a POW! opener.

With a large-group persuasion, you stated the POW! opener matter-of-factly. With a small-group persuasion, the approach is slightly different. Determine first the nature of the problem, opportunity, or weakness. Then find a way to present it that will appeal to the psychology of your bell cow.

To the large group, you said something like: "If we miss the opportunity to put cameras in our cell phones, we will lose a market worth $3 million annually."

If you have determined that the bell cow in a small group is a stability seeker, however, you may want to put it this way: "If we miss the opportunity to put cameras in our cell phones, we will lose our competitive position in this industry."

If you have determined that the bell cow is a change seeker, you may want to put it this way: "If we miss the opportunity to put cameras in our cell phones, we will lose an opportunity to be a leader in a new market that could be a source of major innovations in our industry."

In summary, vary the POW! opener based on psychology:

For Large Group: "If we miss the opportunity to put cameras in our cell phones, we will lose a market worth $3 million annually."

For Stability-Seeking Bell Cow: "If we miss the opportunity to put cameras in our cell phones, we will lose our competitive position in this industry."

For Change-Seeking Bell Cow: "If we miss the opportunity to put cameras in our cell phones, we will lose an opportunity to be a leader in a new market that could be a source of major innovations in our industry."

For a large-group persuasion, you would package your POW! opener as part of a brief story that humanizes the pain your audience is supposed to be feeling. Because the small-group persuasion tends to be less theatrical, the brief story is not necessary. It is enough to describe the pain in a way that it meaningful to the bell cow.

Recommendation

The recommendation step for a small-group persuasion is identical to what it was for a large-group persuasion. It is not some generalized thing like, "Let's all pull together." People dismiss such platitudes out of hand. Your recommendation must be specific, and it must tell the people in the audience what to do. This is not the time to get into details. At this stage of your presentation, your recommendation is a vision of the future; create that vision as simply as possible:

- "We must start making camera phones in time to have them on the shelves before the next buying season."
- "We're going to require a performance guarantee from any shipping vendor that does business with us, and we're going to put a monitoring system in place to measure performance."
- "My recommendation is to tie performance evaluations and bonuses in these two departments to their success in meeting deadlines on the next product rollout."

Benefits

When you get to the section outlining audience benefits, however, you should go back to your psychological profiles. It's important to remember that persuasion is based on benefits specific to the people you're trying to persuade. If it's "good for the company" or creates "a better world," that's just great. But people are most likely to be persuaded by recommendations that help them hold on to their jobs, get promoted, increase their bonuses, expand their influence in the organization, or otherwise benefit them directly.

Saying, "This recommendation will help you hold on to your job" may be too crass for the situation, but if you keep such a benefit in mind, it will help you formulate benefits that bring the person's thinking around to that:

- "This proposal would put your department in the position of directing a major initiative for the company."
- "There's an opportunity here for a savvy manager to grow with this market."
- "This is a lot like the initiative that got _____ her vice presidency."

Support your Recommendation

When you assemble your evidence for the support phase of your presentation, you should keep in mind two things about small group presentations. First, the small group presentation tends to be briefer than the large group presentation. You need to make your points economically. Don't try to preclude questions. Doing so will make you long-winded, and you may be anticipating questions your audience doesn't have. Make sure you know how to answer whatever questions will arise, but don't make use of the knowledge until those questions arise.

Holding back knowledge you have painstakingly assembled can be difficult, but flaunting it for its own sake (which is what you are doing when you try to use your research to prevent questions) will create opportunities for tangential discussions, misunderstandings, and mistakes, any one of which can sabotage a persuasion event.

The second thing you need to keep in mind is that small group presentations tend to be more conversational than large group presentations. When your audience is one to four people, trying to do a formal presentation followed by a structured question and answer session will make you look ridiculous. You must take questions as you go along.

You will still marshal your evidence by the DECISion formula:

- data
- expertise
- cases
- image
- story

As we noted in chapter five, the first, data, is the one used most often in presentations. Data are the statistics and facts that have put so many of us to sleep in the course of someone else's presentation. You need to remember that data is one type of evidence among many, and it's not the most effective type. Pull it all together, then choose a few of your most powerful data points to present. Keep the rest to use in answering questions.

The second type of evidence, expertise, is the opinion of someone your audience will accept as an authority in the subject—an expert, in other words. Expert opinion is valuable if you have it. That's one of the reasons they use it in court during trials.

The third type of evidence, cases, is most useful when you have examples that are close to the experience of your audience members or particularly meaningful to them. Cases or examples are particularly useful because they show real world applications.

The fourth type of evidence, image, is used by way of analogy to relate this new thing (your recommendation) to something familiar. Image is an explanatory form of evidence; it doesn't prove anything. To say that your new centralized production plan operates like the solar system, with Department X in the center, is just a way to help the audience visualize it. Analogies are only suggestive.

The fifth type of evidence, story, is something from your personal experience. It may not readily prove your contentions, but it brings them to life.

Remember, the support step needs to be even briefer than it does in a large-group persuasion. Don't try to overwhelm them with evidence, and plan on presenting your case conversationally.

Action

The last item in the persuasion format is the action step. As we saw in the section on persuading large groups, it is important to give an audience a specific action to take and to put a deadline on that action.

In many presentations, just about any deadline is sufficient. But in a persuasion event the deadline must be immediate, so you can create a constituency for your recommendation. As with a large-group presentation, there is only one deadline for the action step in a small-group presentation:

"Before we leave here today…"

If, as sometimes happens, you're faced with a choice of a major action step later or a more modest one immediately, we recommend the immediate step. At this point, the audience's involvement is more important than the project itself.

CHAPTER **10**

Small Group Showtime

THE SMALL GROUP PERSUASION IS CONVERSATIONAL, AND YOU WILL generally be seated for it. Plan on taking the group's questions as you go along.

Even though you're likely to have much less worry about legibility in your visuals (since the "audience" will be a great deal closer to them), the guidelines for the creation of visuals are the same as they are for large groups. See pages 64-67. Those guidelines are based on communication, not legibility. In short, presenting to a smaller group is no excuse for cramming slides with a lot of text, and the design rules are just as important even when the event is less formal.

Seating

If you control the seating, provide chairs that are moderately padded. Chairs without padding prevent relaxation, especially for thin people. And chairs with generous padding encourage people to fall asleep.

Make sure that the seats all face one another. It is particularly important for you to be able to face each member of the group easily from where you sit. If you need to turn to face anyone (and with a small group, you must make sure you regularly focus on each member), it will be awkward and could throw you off your stride. A circular table would be ideal.

Stance

When you're persuading a small group, you won't be standing, but your posture is still fundamental to your success. Sit straight up and forward in the chair. Keep your hands on the surface of the table, except when you gesture. Gestures are more modest and less expansive than they are when you present to a large group, but they are still necessary.

As with the persuasion of a large group, your message is in your gestures and your facial expressions. Upright, set forward posture is simply a way to keep from distracting the audience from your message.

Eye-Brain Control

Just as in large-group persuasion, where it has roles in both controlling your anxiety and connecting to the audience, eye-brain control is a necessity in small-group presentation. As you speak, look into the eyes of an audience member. Continue to look into that person's eyes until you have completed a thought or sentence, pause, then move your gaze to another person's eyes. It is particularly important with a small group to address everyone in the audience roughly equally.

Eyes have a regulatory effect. Looking at people tends to make them look back at you. Watch the audience's reactions. Don't just observe how they look at you. Observe how they look at each other. This could be the key to determining who the bell cow is, if you don't already know.

When you know who the bell cow is, make use of that knowledge, not by trying to address most of the presentation to that person, but by dealing with that person's questions in an agreeable way. Remember how you wanted to figure out who in the group were change seekers and who were stability seekers? Knowing where the bell cow fits on this scale helps you formulate answers and benefits in ways that are particularly meaningful to that person.

Passion

As with a large group, don't just act passionate about your recommendation; be passionate about it. This is particularly important in a small group persuasion, where conditions are restrictive and your gestures less expansive. You will have to let the feeling come through on its own.

Work with Your Visuals

As with a large group, it's important to "clear the news" when you change a visual. As soon as the visual changes, satisfy the audience's curiosity by telling them what it is and get their attention back to you. We pointed out in the section on large-group persuasion how you must avoid talking to your slides. That advice is even more important in a small group, where talking to your slides is even more noticeable. Whether you are working with a PC or a table-top flip chart, the procedure is this:

- change the visual
- point to the visual with your left hand
- keep your right hand free for gestures
- read the visual (silently) yourself
- turn to the audience
- say what's on the visual
- then go on to discuss what it means.

This is the "Think-Turn-Talk" technique applied in a small group setting.

How to Interact with a Small Group

As we suggested in the previous chapter, you should not plan on a formal question-and-answer session with a small group. When the audience is that small, it's better to conduct the persuasion as a conversation and invite their questions as you go along.

Although you may be tempted to think that an absence of questions means the persuasion is going very well, it isn't. An absence of questions means the audience isn't involved. In order to guarantee their involvement, show them it's OK to talk with you about what you are saying. There is a particular technique for achieving this.

Get the Conversation Going

You have begun with your POW! opener and followed it immediately with your recommendation. The next step is to cite the benefits. But remember, the small group persuasion is conversational in nature. As soon as you have cited the benefits, get the conversation going by asking for a response:

- "What is your reaction so far?"
- "How does this fit with your experience?"

Try to address this specifically to the bell cow, but if you don't know who the bell cow is or the context isn't right for it, then address it to the group in general. Listen carefully to the response. Then use that response as a bridge to the support section:

- "You've raised a good point about the cost. That's why these projections will interest you."
- "It's interesting you should point out the problem of employee morale, because that was one of my major concerns in developing this proposal. Let me show you…"
- "Yes, the timing is critical. I've analyzed that in depth, but since it's the most important issue, let me just make a couple points before I go over it."

While the small-group persuasion resembles a conversation, don't try to treat it like one. At this point, you should have already anticipated most of the other side of the conversation! The persuasion event may not be what you would call scripted, but it is choreographed.

Because you are watching the members of your audience closely, you can detect signs of boredom or see when you are losing them. If either of these happens, ask them for input again or shift to another point. Don't get upset if the mood of the group is such that you think you should abandon some part of your presentation. They will be persuaded by you, not your facts.

A small-group persuasion is a much more personal event than a large-group one, and that makes it more subject to emotions. Anger or resentment that might be hidden in a large group is usually right out in the open in a small group. As with the large group, it's important not to be defensive when you get a challenging question, but it's also more difficult. Use the techniques described in chapter seven for dealing with audience pressure: know the likely issues in advance, listen for the issue in each question, rephrase the question neutrally, answer the issue rather than the challenge, end the answer on a positive note, and tie your answer to a benefit cited in your presentation.

CHAPTER **11**

Be Prepared
to Persuade

THIS CHAPTER IS ABOUT A SPECIALIZED TYPE OF SMALL-GROUP persuasion: impromptu persuasion. There will be times that you see the opportunity to influence people without a formal presentation, and you need to be ready for them.

Mark Twain described how to seize an opportunity when he said, "It usually takes me more than three weeks to prepare a good impromptu speech."

Your opportunities for impromptu persuasion, however, are not going to give you three weeks to prepare. So you need to spend your three weeks up front, before the opportunity to persuade presents itself. That means that you need to invest time thinking about the things you want to persuade people toward. Whenever you come up with an idea for a new strategy, plan, direction, or anything you might need to "sell" to others, think about who benefits and why. Think about ways to organize those benefits into images and figures of speech you will have at your command when you need them.

The Predictable Impromptu Situation

Mark Twain was joking in his comment on impromptu speeches, but a moment's reflection shows there are indeed two kinds of occasions for impromptu persuasion: those you can predict and those you don't expect but want to take advantage of.

How can you predict an occasion for impromptu persuasion? Almost any meeting you attend might be an opportunity. If you know the issues that will be discussed at the meeting, you can prepare yourself on them.

You may not always have to put yourself forward. Often you'll be asked for your input, and that becomes an ideal time to persuade because someone who has asked for your input has indicated receptivity to what you have to say. There are four situations in which your input is likely to be sought:

1. You are viewed as an expert.
2. You are an important person in the organization.
3. You are perceived in the organization as being "on the rise."
4. You have recently had a promotion.

The first two are fairly obvious and may be easy for you to recognize. The third one, that you are perceived as being "on the rise," is a little more subtle. But if you have been marked for advancement somehow, other people in the organization will sense it, and they will often try to ally themselves with you. So you'll find yourself being invited to meetings, and when you attend them you'll be asked for your input.

The fourth situation is less common, but sometimes a promotion means new meetings to attend, and some people at these meetings (maybe even your boss) will take the opportunity to test you.

Looking at the four situations, however, we can see that an able, intelligent, ambitious business professional is likely to spend most of her time in situations conducive to impromptu persuasion. So be prepared. Whenever you are invited to a meeting, ask what it's about. If it's a command performance, you may feel somewhat intimidated about asking. Don't. You have a good reason for asking, "Could you please tell me what the meeting is about so I can be prepared to contribute?"

Format for Impromptu Persuasion

If you can relate a meeting's issue to your recommendation, when the time is right you can say, "I have something I'd like to say about…" Use a tested format to present your recommendation, and in the minute that it takes for you to make your remarks you will not only influence people to your cause, you will be seen as someone with initiative and ideas.

The impromptu persuasion is not as complex as a presentation. Your opener is simple, and you are unlikely to have visuals. After you have asked for the floor by announcing you have something to say or you have been asked for your input, you will make your persuasive case in four parts:

1. Opener
2. Frame the issue
3. Present your point of view
4. Support your position
5. Make your recommendation and cite benefits

Opener. Asking for the floor is your opener: "I have something I'd like to say about..."

Frame the issue. Once you have the floor, you may be tempted to simply rattle off an opinion. Don't. Your initial opinion is not likely to be your best thinking (even if you've tried to prepare!). Furthermore, if someone asks for an opinion and you simply give it, you're playing a subordinate role, responding to a request. This is an opportunity for you to exercise control by framing the issue. Doing so will increase your confidence, buy time to organize your thoughts, and make certain everyone knows what you're talking about.

Let's say someone in the meeting has just given a detailed presentation showing an increased number of missed or delayed shipments in the past quarter. The presenter has also offered evidence that the company's third largest account has taken its business elsewhere, saying it needs reliable shipping. After the presentation your boss, who is at this meeting, asks for your take on it. You're strongly tempted to say something like, "We have to do something about this. We can't stay in business very long if we're losing our major accounts."

But going with whatever's on the top of your head (even if it seems right) is likely to simply repeat whatever was just said, and that means you're not making a contribution. It also means you may miss a chance to persuade those in the meeting to support your proposal to study and overhaul the company's choice of shipper. Before you say anything, look for the issue. When you see it, express it succinctly. "What I see here is that we are losing business because customers are dissatisfied with our shipping."

In many cases your framing may seem obvious, but it's still important. It not only lays out the issue, but it establishes your ownership of it. You are not reacting to someone else's issue, you are discussing your own analysis.

Present your point of view. An impromptu persuasion usually lasts no more than a minute. After you have laid out the issue clearly, the next step is to transition to your contribution on it by briefly stating your point of view. To continue with our example: "I think we should make sure our largest accounts are satisfied with the way their orders are shipped. We cannot continue in business very long if we keep losing our largest customers."

Support your position. As with the formal persuasion events we looked at before, the next step is the largest part of your remarks. In the formal persuasion events we recommended five types of evidence: data, expertise, cases, image, story. Here you will use one type of evidence. This is partly because you probably won't have five types of evidence, but it is mostly because an impromptu persuasion must be brief. The type of evidence you should use is your own professional experience:

"I once worked at a company where one of our suppliers couldn't guarantee delivery schedules on a circuit board we needed for our product. The board was a commodity item, so we contracted with a different manufacturer to ensure we got the boards we needed when we needed them. We never had any problems filling our orders after that. The company that used to supply our boards is no longer in business, by the way."

Your evidence has set up your recommendation, but you must not assume the audience will make the connection on their own. Do it for them by tying the evidence back to the issue: "This tells me that companies won't tolerate uncertainty. If we have already lost one major account, I think we have to assume the rest are at risk as well."

Make your recommendation and cite benefits. Your final step is to present the recommendation you want the audience to adopt: "Here's what I think we should do. First, we should find a shipper that can guarantee performance and is willing to contract with us based on that guarantee. The contract should include penalties when the performance doesn't match the promise. Shipping is a competitive business, and I'm confident we can make such an arrangement. Then, we should offer guaranteed delivery to our customers and promise to compensate them when we miss a target date. If we manage it properly, we can make this compensation equal the shipper's penalty so there's no risk to us. Then we should incorporate the delivery guarantee into our sales and marketing efforts. This way, we will not only stem the loss of customers, but we may be able to turn this situation into a competitive advantage."

Let's see how this impromptu persuasion looks when it's all put together.

Impromptu Persuasion: Making Shipping a Competitive Advantage

I have something I'd like to say about missed and delayed shipments.

What I see here is that we are losing business because customers are dissatisfied with our shipping.

I think we should make sure our largest accounts are satisfied with the way their orders are shipped. We cannot continue in business very long if we keep losing our largest customers.

I once worked at a company where one of our suppliers couldn't guarantee delivery schedules on a circuit board we needed for our product. The board was a commodity item, so we contracted with a different manufacturer to ensure we got the boards we needed when we needed them. We never had any problems filling our orders after that. The company that used to supply our boards is no longer in business, by the way.

This tells me that companies won't tolerate uncertainty. If we have already lost one major account, I think we have to assume the rest are at risk as well.

Here's what I think we should do. First, we should find a shipper that can guarantee performance and is willing to contract with us based on that guarantee. The contract should include penalties when the performance doesn't match the promise. Shipping is a competitive business, and I'm confident we can make such an arrangement. Then, we should offer guaranteed delivery to our customers and promise to compensate them when we miss a target date. If we manage it properly, we can make this compensation equal the shipper's penalty so there's no risk to us. Then we should incorporate the delivery guarantee into our sales and marketing efforts. This way, we will not only stem the loss of customers, but we may be able to turn this situation into a competitive advantage.

Unexpected Persuasion Opportunities

Sometimes, you will find yourself in situations with an unexpected opportunity for persuasion. These will be informal occasions. They won't be meetings, because you have prepared yourself for those. They will ordinarily be one-to-one conversations. You will see an opportunity to bring the conversation around to your recommendation and influence another person to support your cause. How do you handle these opportunities?

Unexpected persuasion opportunities don't fit into a fixed format. They are more a matter of style than structure. First of all, look for the benefit. No matter what else goes into the persuasion, listener benefit is the single most powerful persuader.

It's generally not enough to simply offer the benefit, however. If you are trying to persuade someone to adopt a new position or point of view, you must usually help him overcome a great deal of inertia, even if he will realize a substantial benefit by doing so. You overcome this inertia by raising his comfort level with the new position. Since you represent the new position, this means raising his comfort level with you.

Listen Actively

First of all, in order to package your recommendation as a benefit you must listen actively to what a person says. Active listening has two benefits for persuasion: 1) it helps you get information about a person's goals so you can align your recommendation with them, and 2) it makes the person feel comfortable with you.

Active listening is more than a phrase. It is an actual technique. It has four parts:
- be attentive
- detect and acknowledge feelings
- play back information
- ask open-ended questions.

Be attentive. It may sound obvious, but the first step in active listening is to listen. Attentiveness in this context means listening without making judgments, which you must do in order to get the other person's message clearly. Pay attention to everything she says. Make notes if you want to. In many conversational situations making notes may seem strange, and you have to judge that for yourself. But very few people feel anything but flattered to have someone make notes about what they say.

Detect and acknowledge feelings. By listening carefully, you should be able to hear the emotional component in another person's conversation. Watch body language, listen to voice tone. When you detect feeling in the person's conversation, acknowledge it and try to describe the feeling specifically (don't just identify the feelings as "good" or "bad"):

- "That must make you feel frustrated."
- "That must have been disappointing for you."
- "You must have been proud about that."

Play back information. Repeat in your own words what the person has said to you. This lets the person know you have understood what she said and gives her the opportunity to correct misunderstandings. You can cue the other person that you're about to play back with a phrase like, "Let me see if I understand you correctly…" Then replay what the person just told you and use your own words to show that you've processed it. Using your own words is important. Otherwise, you'll just be parroting the person.

Ask open-ended questions. Finally, question the speaker to encourage him to provide more information. But don't use yes-no questions. Don't ask, for example, "Is this different from the way they do it in the other department?" Ask, "How is this different from the way they do it in the other department?"

Active listening helps you gather important information, but it does much more than that. It raises a person's comfort level with you. The simple fact is, you cannot listen actively without being interested in what the person is saying. The more actively you listen, the more interested you are. People are always more comfortable with others who are interested in them. It's human nature.

Raise the Comfort Level

By listening actively to the other person, you have gathered information you may need to package your recommendation as a benefit to that person. And you have begun the process of raising that person's comfort level with you. It is possible to boost this comfort level even further.

Pacing and leading is a technique that grew out of the work of hypnotherapist Milton Erickson, who studied the importance of gaining rapport in both therapy and hypnotism. Erickson found that by increasing rapport, a therapist could raise a client's receptiveness to suggestion. You won't be hypnotizing people, of course, but you can use some of Erickson's techniques to help put another person at ease and free him from distractions that can prevent his decision to embrace your proposal.

Here's a brief scenario that shows how pacing works. You see a friend walking down the street. You catch up to her, say "hello," and walk beside her, matching her pace. When she returns your greeting you match your first conversational remark to the volume and tone of her voice. When she gestures, you emphasize your remarks with similar gestures. Adopt her posture. As she speaks, you listen, and when you speak, you match the speed as well as the tone and volume of her conversation. Now you are walking at her pace, mirroring her gestures, using her posture, and speaking to her at the same volume, speed, and tone that she speaks.

Now gradually slow your pace. If you are sufficiently gradual, she will slow her pace to match yours. In fact, you have now established rapport with her, and she would probably be more receptive to your recommendation now than she would otherwise. Notice how you did it: by paying attention to her—her voice, gestures, posture, and pace. Pacing and leading requires you to make a study of the person you want to put at ease. You can't do it without being truly interested in the person, which is probably one of the reasons why it works so well.

Now apply it to a typical work situation, which will probably be an office. Try to arrange for it to be the other person's office rather than yours, since your goal is to make the other person comfortable. Match your posture to that of the other person. Don't mimic the other person's gestures, but give yours similar scope and intensity. Match the tone and volume of your speech to his conversation. Watch his breathing and match the speed of your speech to it.

Now introduce this variation: watch what he does and suggest that he do it. If he looks away and stares into space or at the wall, say, "Let's think about this for a minute." If he writes something, say, "Let's make a note of this."

Above all, however, listen to what he says, and listen actively. Find his concerns, goals, needs, and aspirations and align your recommendation with them. Then gradually bring the conversation in that direction, just as if you were slowing down a little while walking with him and trying to get him to match your pace.

Pacing and leading is a technique often used by sales professionals, particularly for big-ticket products like cars and time-sharing condos. Some people view it, then, as a coercive or manipulative tactic. In reality, however, effective pacing requires such concentration on the subject that it is extremely difficult to do without sincerity. And in fact, Milton Erickson, whose work it is based on, developed his techniques specifically as a way to respect his patients and give them a choice about accepting help.

PART IV
Persuading Virtual Groups

CHAPTER

12

A Non-Technical Look at Communication Technology

MCI's NATIONAL STUDY OF BUSINESS TRAVEL AND communications, *Meetings in America V*, found that three-quarters of respondents (the sample was broadly representative of business types) had participated in a web conference in the 12 months preceding the study (August, 2003). The figure was even higher (87%) for senior executives. Another study from Wainhouse Research showed that 75% of business travelers felt more productive with conferencing services than in-person meetings.

Such findings should send signals to anyone who is excessively attached to in-person communication. The senior executive figure is especially telling, because if senior executives are eager to embrace distance communication technologies, junior executives (and anyone else in an organization) may have little chance of avoiding them.

The pace at which distance communications technologies are being installed is accelerating, too. These days, you can buy a "web cam" for under $200 and begin something that resembles videoconferencing for the cost of an Internet connection and some instant messaging software. One sign that computer-based videoconferencing is becoming more affordable is the emergence of charitable organizations that make the technology available to military families, which often have limited resources. An organization called the Freedom Calls Foundation, for example, began offering video communication in the summer of 2004 between military people in Iraq and Afghanistan and their families back in the U.S. without charge.

Is the growing ubiquity of distance communication technologies good news or bad news for would-be persuaders? Up to this point, we have tried to show that you are your own most important tool of persuasion. If your presence is reduced to a voice in a speaker or an image on a screen, this is bound to limit your ability to persuade. Although the technology that conveys your voice and image grows more capable all the time, it will be a long time before anyone develops a convincing way to shake hands at a distance. So it is safe to say that attempting to persuade someone without being present is always going to have some limitations.

Professional persuaders understand these limitations implicitly. The Meetings in America V study, for example, found marketing and sales professionals to have the least interest in web conferencing. They were also least likely to have attended a web conference and, by a very large margin, least likely to have led one. The people who most trade in persuasion, in other words, are the last to embrace distance communication technologies.

On the other hand, we don't have much choice but to use these technologies. As they grow less expensive, more effective, and more available, they will inevitably establish themselves as the standard for business communication. Live meetings will become less and less frequent and more difficult to justify. So it makes sense for us to learn how best to use communication technologies in the service of persuasion.

Communication Channels

There are three basic channels of communication: sound, sight, and data. When you and your visuals meet an audience in person, you and your audience use all three seamlessly. When communicating at a distance, however, the channels are separated. Furthermore, they do not always operate both ways. The greatest limitation of distance technologies for persuasion is your inability to gauge audience reaction, for with any audience over a handful of people and anything less than full-duplex video and sound communication, most of the audience's reaction will be closed to you. This makes audience-based communication, which is the essence of persuasion, fairly problematic.

Choosing the technology you will use to persuade means finding the most cost-effective combination of sound, sight, and data in what you have available.

Sound. Sound is carried by telephone, and that makes it the most commonly available communications channel. Every business organization has a telephone line, and in these days of cell and satellite phones, telephone access is literally everywhere. Sound, then, is the baseline communications channel. You can nearly always plan on having it. Persuading an audience via teleconference is not as easy as doing it in person, or even via video. But there are things you can do to make it more effective than it otherwise would be.

Sight. Motion images are carried by video, and a video signal can also include sound. Video access, however, is much more limited than telephone access. Until recently it nearly always required a studio, which is why videoconferencing was generally done in videoconferencing centers (and still is, for formal or high-end applications). But two-way analog videoconferencing with large screens, high-fidelity sound, and a computer connection for your visuals is the next best thing to being there. For critical persuasion events, then, consider high-end videoconferencing. You can apply most of what you have read in this book about persuading large groups.

Data. Data is, of course, carried by computers over networking and telephone connections. With the advent of the web, data communications can go nearly anywhere, and access is nearly as ubiquitous as it is with the telephone. You can therefore make a PowerPoint file available to nearly anyone simply by uploading it to a website. A PowerPoint file without a presenter, however, is about as persuasive as a handout without a presenter, which is to say not persuasive at all. But you cannot convey a presentation over a network connection the way you can over a video signal. There is simply too much data, and even the broadest of broadband connections will choke on a raw video signal.

Sound and sight, however, can be compressed into data streams small enough to move comfortably over network connections. A video camera and a microphone can collect video and audio and turn them over to the computer system, which then compresses them and sends the compressed data to the other computer, which decompresses it and presents it to the audience as audio and video. The software that accomplishes this compression and decompression is called a codec.

Codecs require substantial computing horsepower. But desktop computers and their operating systems are so powerful these days that most computer users can afford to run some type of videoconferencing. And this has revolutionized business meetings in just the past few years. Almost any business can afford to set up a computer-based videoconferencing facility, and almost any user can learn to operate it effectively.

CHAPTER 13

Analyzing "Virtual" Audiences

NO MATTER HOW INTERACTIVE YOUR TECHNOLOGY, persuading at a distance will always be at a disadvantage compared to persuading in person. There will be limits to how well you can read the audience's reaction, and with large audiences—where you're likely to be using one-way or broadcast technology—you probably won't be able to read it at all.

But you can't persuade without an audience-centered approach. So being audience-centered may have more to do with content than delivery. Think hard about audience benefits and emphasize them as much as you can.

Your Audience

You will certainly have less anxiety about presenting to an audience that isn't there than you would about presenting to a roomful of people. This may make you feel more comfortable, but it has disadvantages, too. With less tension, you may have to work harder to keep yourself excited, and you will need to stay excited in order to get your audience excited. Paradoxically, the cure for the lack of excitement is the same as the cure for anxiety: concentrate on your goal. You're excited about winning this audience over, right? You must keep reminding yourself of that. What do you want these people to do as a result of your presentation? You might even try visualizing them doing it.

Everything we said about goals with large audiences and small audiences applies to "virtual" audiences as well. State your goal with an active verb—adopt, reject, decide, move, change, reverse—and focus on what you are trying to accomplish.

This table, reproduced from chapter four, has some sample goal statements designed to show the difference between those for an informational presentation and those for a persuasive presentation.

When my presentation is over, I want the audience to...

Informational presentation	Persuasive presentation
...understand my department's position on the new marketing plan.	...reject the new marketing plan.
...know how to read a quality analysis report.	...adopt the continuous quality improvement method.
...remember the importance of radio advertising in the marketing mix.	...change the marketing mix to give radio a 25% larger share.

Put your written statement of your goal somewhere you will see it while you're preparing your presentation. Compare every point you make to that goal. If the point doesn't seem to support the goal, reconsider it. When your goal is persuasion, a briefer presentation is nearly always better than a longer one. And when your venue is virtual, brevity assumes an even greater importance.

The reason brevity is so important in virtual venues is because the venue is inherently boring! Human beings are by nature social creatures. Their attention is attracted and held by other human beings. For proof of this, try this thought experiment. You're watching an engrossing program on television. A stranger walks into the room. What does that do to your focus? The vast majority of human beings will notice and attend to the stranger in some way, even if they don't turn to look. We can't help it. People are inherently interesting to us.

So when you are persuading by telephone or video, it will take more of your energy to get the attention of participants and it will take more energy on their part to give it. That means keeping your presentation short. If for some reason you must make the presentation long, build in breaks. How long is "long"? Much of human activity is built on the standard of the hour. Most meetings are planned for an hour; most classes are an hour long. But meetings and classes feature live human beings, so don't plan on 60 minutes of uninterrupted persuasion in a virtual venue. Fifty minutes is probably the maximum; 30-40 minutes would be better.

Audience Analysis for a Virtual Group

In the chapters on large group and small group persuasion, we offered a scoring system to determine toughness of the "room." You can go back to chapter four if you want to review audience responsiveness. The standards (size of audience, priority of subject, attention span, identity of decision makers, and impact of benefits) are the same. But because virtual venues are inherently boring, and your physical presence is so limited, you will do best by simply assuming that any "room" in a virtual venue is extremely tough. That means your best strategy is to focus your presentation on audience benefits and supporting evidence.

The audience analysis worksheet for a virtual venue is the same as it is for a live meeting, except it has two additional questions related to the technology.

Audience Analysis Worksheet—Virtual Venue

1. How many people will attend the meeting?
2. Why are they attending?
3. What is their relationship to the meeting?
4. Do they know each other?
5. What organization(s) do they come from?
6. What are their job functions?
7. What is their "rank" in relation to yours?
8. What is their general level of knowledge about the topic?
9. What is the range of their ages?
10. What is the gender mix?
11. What is the cultural diversity?
12. What is their primary language?
13. What do they have in common with you?
14. How do they feel about the position you want to persuade them to?
15. What are their aspirations?
16. What are their fears?
17. What is their technological skill level in the meeting's medium?
18. How are they going to connect to the event?

In chapter eight, we explained how to analyze the psychology of a small audience. If your virtual venue audience is small, the same concepts apply. If it is large, you won't be able to analyze individuals sufficiently to make any difference.

As we noted, however, audience benefits are paramount when persuading in a virtual venue. So put as much effort as possible into answering the question we have raised again and again: What's in it for the audience?

14

Structuring a Presentation to Persuade in a Virtual Venue

WE SAW IN THE SECTIONS ON LARGE GROUP AND SMALL GROUP persuasion that there is a temptation for would-be persuaders to think the PowerPoint file is the presentation. That tendency is even more marked when you are trying to persuade in a virtual venue. Your presence will be reduced to a voice in a speaker or an image on a screen. You will be comparable in size to your visuals, and you won't have the offset of your physical presence to demand attention. At worst, then, you may become to the audience just another piece of technology: the one that controls the slides.

Make the best visuals you can for your persuasion event, but don't fall into the trap of thinking they will carry you. If it is difficult to move a roomful of people to your point of view, how much more difficult must it be when they are sitting in their own offices, surrounded by both the pressures and the comforts that drive organizational inertia?

Our format for live persuasion was five steps. The format for persuasion in a virtual venue is very similar, but it has quite a few more steps, designed to keep you in control of the technology:

- Introduction
- Ground Rules
- Attention Getter
- Recommendation
- Benefits
- Support

- Recommendation Restatement
- Action
- Transitions.

Introduction

The introduction is no more than two sentences. In one sentence you introduce yourself and describe your credentials, if necessary. In the second sentence, you introduce the topic.

Ground Rules

In a virtual venue, it's important to establish at the outset how the technology will be used. Explain what features will be used, how participants ask for recognition of their questions or comments, how questions will be handled (save them for the end, even with a small group), that questioners need to identify themselves by name and location, and so forth.

Attention Getter

In live persuasion, we recommended the POW! (for problem, opportunity, or weakness) opener. Although the meeting has been underway for two steps already, you need to focus the audience's attention at this point, and you can do that with a POW! statement. Follow it quickly with a brief positioning statement on the audience's interest in the matter: "The company's future depends on manufacturing camera phones."

Recommendation

This is where you share with the audience your objective: "We must adopt the new marketing plan in order to maintain our position in the industry."

Benefits

You have already suggested the audience's interest in this recommendation during your Attention Getter. Here is where you provide a more detailed, but still brief, statement of how they will benefit from your recommendation. Remember, this is a statement of how members of the audience will benefit, not how you will benefit, not how the organization will benefit, not how the industry will benefit. While the audience may benefit if the organization, industry, or nation benefits, draw the personal connection for them. Don't expect them to do it on their own.

Support

Here is where you present your evidence. Remember the DECISion spectrum of evidence: data, expertise, cases, image, and story. Whatever forms of evidence you use, try to personalize them. Even in a virtual venue, personalization is more appealing than numbers and faceless cases. Keep it brief. Don't try to prevent their questions. In fact, it makes sense to leave certain areas of the case open. If you give participants a reason to ask questions, it will raise their energy and awareness levels.

Recommendation Restatement

This part is two sentences. The first sentence is a brief restatement of your recommendation. The second is a brief restatement of the principal benefit to the audience.

Action

This is a specific action item you want audience members to do. It needs to have a deadline, and for purposes of persuasion, the best deadline is immediate: "Before we leave here today…"

Transitions

In live persuasion, as you move from step to step in the presentation, your presence unifies it. If you simply stand in silence for a few seconds you nevertheless maintain continuity, and the audience waits expectantly. Transitions, in other words, are not necessary. But persuasion in a virtual venue can be subject to what those who work in radio call "dead air." A silent second on the radio throws the entire studio into a panic. Radio people know that silence loses listeners. If you're listening to the radio and the broadcast goes silent, even for two seconds, you will probably change the station, if for no other reason than to make sure the radio is working properly. This may happen at a less intense level in a teleconference, videoconference, or webconference, but it will still happen.

As the persuader, then, you need to prevent silences by creating transition statements that will fill air time even while each step is sinking in and you are preparing to deliver the next one. Good transitions give your presentation a better flow and make it seem more professional, too.

Rehearsal

As you no doubt expect, rehearsal is every bit as important for persuasion in a virtual venue as it is for persuasion in person. But it has an additional step: run through it with the equipment. You will not be persuasive unless you are in complete command of the equipment. It's not enough to read an instruction book. You actually need to "drive" it before your presentation. Doing this won't guarantee you a smooth presentation, but it will at least eliminate one source of difficulty.

When you are doing your technological run-through, make sure your test audience includes someone whose connection speed is as slow as the slowest connection you expect to find in the regular audience for your presentation. Note where the lags are and plan something to fill them.

CHAPTER 15

Virtual Venue Showtime

PERSUADING IN A VIRTUAL VENUE REQUIRES JUST AS MUCH friendliness as live persuasion. In fact, it requires more, because you must be friendly to the equipment as well as the audience. Wear neutral, solid colors for video. Avoid red. Minimize reflective or fluorescent decoration, like trendy pins or sparkling jewelry.

Require participants to introduce themselves at the start of the meeting and whenever they speak. Beware of a transmission delay and pause to let participants speak.

Eye Contact

If your meeting uses two-way video technology, it is important to maintain eye contact with participants. Strangely enough, you do this not by looking into the other person's eyes, but by looking into the lens of the video camera. So it's important to mount the camera at a distance sufficient to let you look into the camera lens and the video screen (or computer monitor) at the same time. Otherwise you'll be looking away from the camera to look at the image of the other person, which breaks eye contact.

Passion

In a teleconference, you should use posture and gestures the way you would for an in-person event. This is one of the ways you play the role of confident speaker, and when you act like a confident speaker, you become one.

In a videoconference, however, sudden or excessive movement taxes the codec, so that your image can have dropped frames or video artifacts. So when you're on computer-based video, you should not move fast or suddenly. In fact, it's better to minimize movement altogether. This means you must convey much of your presence with facial expressions and voice tone.

Vary the pitch of your voice—more pitch variation means more auditory stimuli. This makes it easier for listeners to focus on the sound. Keep within an acceptable decibel range. In live presentation, we suggested you should always be louder than normal conversation. That may not be the case for persuading in virtual venues. Check the capacities of the equipment. You want to be loud enough to be heard without distorting the sound (or the meaning) of your words. Say words clearly—pronounce all syllables, especially the final consonants. Speak at a moderate rate—fast enough to maintain attention without rushing. Use pauses for emphasis and clarity—separate phrases and give your audience time to comprehend your meaning.

Use common terminology—keep your words within a vocabulary range that the audience understands. Keep your sentences short—10 to 15 words per sentence is a good average. Be realistic—use language that reflects reality and is precise. Exaggeration can be deadly to your credibility. Check for understanding—ask questions to make sure that the listeners received the meaning behind your words.

Work with Your Visuals

As with in-person audiences, it's important to "clear the news" when you change the visual. As soon as the visual changes, satisfy the audience's curiosity by telling them what it is and get their attention back to you. If you need to look away from the camera to see your visuals, you should follow a procedure very similar to the "Think-Turn-Talk" method outlined for in-person audiences:

- Satisfy curiosity. Clear the news from the visual.
- Read off bullet points from top to bottom. THEN elaborate on any point that requires it.
- For a line chart, identify the title, the horizontal and vertical axes, and the trend lines.
- For diagrams, drawings, or photos, give an overview of the content.

- Assume the visual is new material for everyone looking at it, even if it's old news to you.

Don't assume everybody is looking at the same part of the visual. And don't assume everyone in the audience understands how your graph is set up.

Because of bandwidth variations and modem speeds, you can encounter a delay of up to 15 seconds between the time you click for your next visual and when it appears on participants' screens. In order to avoid gaps in your presentation, manage your transitions:

- Plan a transition for each visual and write it into your notes.
- Take a brief question before you click to the next visual and use the gap to give a concise answer.
- Check in with participants to make sure they're still connected and involved.
- Ask for confirmation of your point from a specific participant.
- Summarize information given previously, if appropriate.

Make sure you don't move on to the next visual before the current one arrives on everyone's screen. Don't take questions between visuals that require long answers; otherwise, you'll still be answering the question when the next visual arrives, and it will interfere with clearing the news. Vary your transition statements.

Here are four types of transitions:

- Question. "How are you feeling about…"
- Factoid. "By the way, did you know that…"
- Silence. Use this one carefully.
- Check-in. "Tom, let me know when you see…"

How to Interact with a Virtual Group

There are many ways in which persuaders are at a disadvantage when trying to persuade audiences that are not there in person. But at least one of these formats—web conferencing—makes up for these disadvantages with one large advantage. Most web conferencing platforms include a polling feature. When presenting in person, you can sometimes get a sense of the group by asking for a show of hands in response to a question, but then you are distracted by counting them. With polling, you can ask questions and get instant responses, all tallied. What better way to find out what's in it for the audience?

If participants...	Then try to...
Ramble	Interrupt politely by paraphrasing information and how it connects to your objective. Then return to the agenda.
Monopolize the interactions	Recognize their enthusiasm as positive, table their input as a "good point," then ask for other responses.
Are off topic	Thank them for the input and ask to move the discussion off-line. Refer to the time costraints and the objectives when necessary.
Make no sense	Avoid embarrassing them. Try to make a concise response and move on. If there seems to be a good point in there somewhere, ask a clarifying question.
Become a distraction (background noise, connecting and reconnecting, etc.)	Politely ask "Whoever is…" to stop the behavior. Don't name them. They may not be aware they are causing difficulties.
Are true experts	• Recognize them (publicly during the meeting or privately beforehand). • Make them part of your plan and ask for their input where you want it.
Think they are experts	Recognize their interest and enthusiasm, but table their comments as appropriate. If they make statements that are wrong, do not agree with them.
Are hostile	• Agree to disagree and move on. • Remain calm. • Agree with and focus on any part of the criticism that's true. • Rephrase the question.

Audiences in virtual venues can sometimes be difficult, perhaps even more so than in-person audiences. People in an in-person audience may be more constrained in their behavior and less likely to confront you. But sometimes, despite your audience analysis, your ground rules, and your preparation, an audience will surprise you. This table shows some difficult situations that can take can take place in virtual venue meetings and offers suggestions for handling them.

In many ways, you manage a virtual audience in the same way you manage an in-person one. Review techniques in the chapters on small and large groups.

CHAPTER **16**

Tips for Persuading in Virtual Venues

THE THREE VIRTUAL VENUES—TELECONFERENCING, videoconferencing, and web-based videoconferencing—each have particular characteristics that influence communication. This chapter is a collection of tips for managing the different venues to make them as conducive to persuasion as possible.

Teleconferencing

The telephone is hard to beat for reliable, clear conversation. And teleconferencing is a mature technology and industry. We can expect it to remain viable for a long time, particularly for information-based communication, such as press conferences, the presentation of financial results to analysts, and so forth. In addition, the teleconference is probably the cheapest meeting you can hold. It's even cheaper than in-person meetings, since you need to provide neither meeting space nor refreshments.

Show Visuals Via the Web. You cannot present yourself as much more than a disembodied voice in a teleconference, but at least you can provide your visuals, either as a handout you send ahead of time or via web conference. You may remember that we recommended distributing handouts only after the meeting is over, to avoid the problem of the audience studying the handout rather than listening to you. So if you have a choice between providing handouts physically or showing visuals via web conference, take the web conference. It will give you greater control and make you better able to clear the news for each new slide.

Set Some Rules. One-way teleconferencing and large-group teleconferencing are both unsuited to persuasion because of the absence or difficulty of audience interaction. This means your teleconferencing persuasion event will likely be a small group. Require that each person give a self-introduction (name, title, location) at the beginning of the meeting, and require that each person say her name before speaking.

Use Stance and Voice. During your remarks stand straight and balanced, just as if you were presenting to a roomful of people. Make your gestures. Speak loudly and clearly. You can see we are advising you to conduct a persuasion event by telephone in much the same way you would in person. There are two reasons for this. One is psychological, in that acting like you are in an in-person meeting will make you feel more like you are in an in-person meeting, which will give you more control. The other reason is physical. Standing up and gesturing with your arms will increase the volume of your voice.

Set up a mirror where you can use it to observe yourself. This will help you keep your facial expression friendly and enthusiastic. Most telephone users, whether they identify it or not, can "hear" facial expressions. Just ask anyone who does telephone sales.

Use a headset. It will be much easier to follow all these suggestions if you run the meeting with a headset rather than a telephone handset.

Secure the Area. You will probably be conducting your teleconference from your office. Take steps to make sure there are no interruptions. Disable the ringer on your telephone, lock your door, or do whatever you can to prevent intrusive sounds that could disrupt your concentration or excite the curiosity of your audience.

Use the Mute Button. In order to keep the world outside until the persuasion is finished, ask audience members to minimize noise: typing, office noise, and so forth. If they can't stop the noise, they can block it out with the mute button. They can take off the muting when they want to ask questions. Alternatively, ask your teleconferencing company if there is a mute function available to you as the speaker. This is more difficult to deal with, since it will be up to you to release the muting, and you will have no way of knowing when they want to comment or have questions. If you have a web conference going at the same time, they can signal you. If not, you may be able to reserve certain parts of your remarks during which there will be no input.

Use Humor with Care. In a teleconference, audience members will not be able to see your face and may not know when you are joking.

Videoconferencing

Video may be the next best thing to being there, but you need to keep in mind that you aren't there, and you cannot run a video persuasion just like a live one.

Show Visuals Via the Web. As with the teleconference, you're better off controlling your visuals rather than distributing them ahead of time. Don't assume you can present them on-camera as you would in person. They won't look good as "second generation" images, and using a second camera so they displace your image on the screen isn't good because it takes the attention off you. So present the visuals on a separate channel, over the web. Clear the news the same way you would in a live meeting.

Set Some Rules. Again, whether your videoconference is one-way or both ways, you want to make this as interactive as possible. Require that each person give a self-introduction (name, title, location) at the beginning of the meeting, and require that each person say her name before speaking, unless she is appearing on the screen.

Use Stance and Voice. Because you need to remain in view of the camera, you may not be able to stand up. If that's the case, use the posture from the small-group persuasion procedure: sit up straight, keep you hands on top of the table, reduce the expansiveness of your gestures. Hold gestures a "beat" longer than you would in a live meeting. Rapid gestures don't come across well on camera.

Check your camera position. Make sure you are eye level with the camera, and make sure you are far enough away from it so your features aren't distorted with a fisheye effect. If your conference is two-way, you need to make sure you can look at the incoming image and the camera lens at the same time. If your gaze doesn't hit the camera directly while you are watching the screen, you will look distracted.

Know the Equipment. Make sure all the devices have fresh batteries. Know the best placement for the camera and the microphones. If you can, use the equipment before the persuasion event. See what you look like on camera.

Mind the Lighting. Use indirect lighting. Anything else will create excessive shadows on your face. Know that some types of fluorescent lights will make you appear green. Make sure no white background can be seen. If you can paint all your walls blue, that will work best.

Dress Carefully. Narrow horizontal stripes may be of the same scale as the video scan lines and will create a moiré pattern. Any busy pattern on your clothing will suffer over video and look distracting to the audience. Solid colors are best. Light gray will make your skin look tan. Blue or violet will make it look pink. White will make you look very dark. Dark clothing works best.

Optimize Your Environment. Offices tend to have a lot of glass—in windows, on picture frames, on top of desks—and glass can be terrible acoustically. Make sure glass surfaces are angled downward or covered up so they won't reflect sound.

To humanize the way you come across on video, put up a sign in the background that says where you are and arrange to have a potted plant in the participants' field of view. Even an artificial plant will work.

Web-Based Videoconferencing

In general, you should use the videoconferencing tips for web-based videoconferencing as well. But web-based videoconferencing has its own limitations.

Avoid Extraneous Motion. Any movement in the image you are presenting activates the codec's compression algorithms. If there is too much movement the codec cannot keep up, and it will drop frames or show intrusive blocks known as video artifacts in the picture. It is not simply the case that you must limit your own motions (which of course limits your expressiveness), but you must take care not to have any extraneous motion in the scene you are presenting. The sweeping second hand of a clock in the background or a potted plant swaying in an errant breeze will make you less persuasive by reducing the software's capacity to convey your image with fidelity.

The best way to get good fidelity in a computer-based video image is to reduce yourself to a talking head. But then you lose the expressiveness of your gestures and the authority of your posture—it's a trade-off.

Mind the Delay. Because the codec must compress the video, send it, then decompress it at the other end, there is almost a guarantee of a delay, no matter how fast the various computers in the meeting are. So take special care not to talk over others, and let the meeting participants know how many problems will be created by interruptions and cross-talk.

Be Prepared for Internet Weather. Have you ever been to a website you visit regularly and found that it wouldn't load? Have you ever had to wait several hours for an email message you knew was on its way to you? The Internet cannot be disabled by traffic, vandalism, or sabotage, but it is subject to "storms." It's possible your meeting can be momentarily interrupted or garbled by forces completely beyond your control, and such interruptions may be more likely over the web than they would be by video hookup or the telephone. This is one reason it is good to connect the conference by telephone as well as the web.

PART V
A History of Persuasion

CHAPTER 17

Whatever Happened to Rhetoric?

IN THE MODERN AGE OF ADVERTISING AND PROPAGANDA, we are tempted to think that persuasion is a new phenomenon. But it is as old as human society, and it actually has an interesting history. This chapter hits some of the highlights of that history for readers who have an interest.

As a formal discipline, persuasion is at least 2,400 years old, but informally it is probably as old as speech itself. Persuasion is a branch of a larger field of study called rhetoric, which is the study of effective speaking and writing. It takes its name from the Greek word "rhetor," or "orator."

Today the term "rhetoric," at least in popular usage, is somewhat disparaging. In political discussions, we often characterize the other side of the argument as "mere rhetoric." When someone speaks a question for which no answer is expected, we call it "rhetorical." We never speak kindly about a person's rhetoric, and underlying most of our discussions on substantive communication is an ideal that involves the exchange of ideas without the interference of rhetoric. When we looked it up in the dictionary, we learned it is "the undue use of exaggeration or display."

It has been a long way down for rhetoric, which 2,400 years ago was one of the three liberal arts (the others being logic and grammar). For about 2,000 years, it was the most important field of study a human being could undertake. But it steadily lost importance after the Middle Ages until the 20th century, when interest revived as people tried to understand how rhetoric works in mass communication.

Aristotle and the Three Rhetorical Proofs

The earliest mention of rhetoric in literature was in the works of Plato, who suggested (around 385 B.C.) that rhetoric was dangerous. He believed it was the foremost of the arts. But he said mastering it would enable a man to dominate the affairs of a community, whether or not he had truth on his side. Plato considered this possibility not only dangerous but morally wrong. So he anticipated most of our modern feelings about it.

Plato's student, Aristotle, in trying to find a rhetoric that might be morally acceptable, became the most important figure in the history of western rhetoric.

Aristotle described the distinction between content and delivery. He further said that persuasion relies on "proofs," of which there are three kinds:

- reasoning
- emotion
- the character and credibility of the persuader.

Nobody has ever done a better job of clarifying the three types of persuasion, but it's important to note that the three types of appeal generally work together to achieve persuasion. Some of these may feel instinctive when we develop them for a presentation. Thus, we will usually introduce ourselves and state our interest in the topic in order to promote our credibility: "I've been in public relations for ten years and I've seen a lot of ideas come and go." And while we generally try to make reasoning the centerpiece of our attempts to persuade, we also try to present it in emotional terms: "How many people would we have to lay off to cover a $250,000 shortfall?"

Note that when we are persuaded, we usually experience Aristotle's three proofs seamlessly. We generally even delude ourselves that emotional appeals and appeals to character are incapable of moving us, that we are only persuaded by the reasoning. Yeah, right.

Cicero Explains the Arrangement of the Appeals

Aristotle's philosophy of persuasion was destined to remain in place for about 1,400 years, and those who followed him merely introduced refinements. One of the first refinements was organizing rhetoric into five areas of study:

- invention (finding something to say)
- arrangement (ordering the points of the presentation)
- style (expressing ideas artfully)
- memory (more than memorization, memory also includes strategies for mentally storing a presentation and for making it memorable to the audience)
- delivery (the Greeks called it hypokrisis, or "acting").

Today we no longer think of these five areas as fields of study, but they remain with us as types of preparation for a persuasion event. Some persuaders go through them sequentially, in just the order they appear above. Other persuaders take a more holistic approach, combining invention and arrangement or style and memory or memory and invention. Not everybody thinks the same way, and when you seek to persuade people, you will be most effective when you use the preparation method with which you're most comfortable. That's one of the reasons practice is so important to persuasion; it provides the opportunities to try on different ways of preparing.

Cicero, the greatest of Roman orators, did important work in the third field of study, arrangement. He created a template for an oration by dividing it into six steps: introduction, statement of facts, goal of speech, proof, refutation, and conclusion. Cicero used different names for the six steps, but we have translated them into something that makes sense for modern readers. He then sorted Aristotle's three "proofs" (reason, emotion, and character) into these categories:

Steps	Appeal
1. Introduction	Character
2. Statement of facts	Reason
3. Goal of speech	Reason
4. Proof	Reason
5. Refutation	Reason
6. Conclusion	Emotion

Cicero, then, advised the persuader to rely on character in the introduction, reason in all the intermediary steps, and emotion in the conclusion. If you look at some of the speeches found in the appendix of this book (all of which were delivered thousands of years after Cicero), you will see that public speakers and orators continue to follow his template, although many omit some of the intermediate steps. But they nearly all start with character, move to reason, and conclude with emotion. It's a good structure to keep in mind. We think of it as the three c's:

- present your Character
- make your Case
- strike an emotional Chord.

You can see this pattern, for example, in Abraham Lincoln's Second Inaugural Address. When Lincoln was inaugurated for his second term as President, he faced a difficult situation. The country was in a civil war that had begun as the suppression of a rebellion and had evolved into a crusade to eliminate slavery. Lincoln's Emancipation Proclamation the year before this inauguration had made the new war aims official. He now found himself leading a citizenry weary of war and often doubting the value of the antislavery crusade. He had to take every opportunity to renew the country's commitment to it.

He began by presenting himself and his character, explaining why he was going to speak only briefly: "Fellow countrymen: At this second appearing to take the oath of the presidential office, there is less occasion for an extended address than there was at the first."

In making his case, he disarmed his audience with utter frankness, declaring he had no news to report on the conduct of the war and that they knew as well as he how it was going. He hoped they felt the news was encouraging, he said, but "with high hope for the future, no prediction in regard to it is ventured."

He reminded everyone how inevitably the war had descended on them and reminded them of the tension during his previous inauguration, when "insurgent agents were in the city seeking to destroy it without war—seeking to dissolve the Union, and divide effects, by negotiation."

Neither the North nor the South, he said, expected the war to be as intense or as long as it had been. Both regions read the same Bible and pray to the same God, and each calls on God's help against the other. Then he let his sense of irony remind his audience of what the other side stood for, even while he reaffirmed his side's sense of Christian decency: "It may seem strange that any men should dare to ask a just God's assistance in wringing their bread from the sweat of other men's faces; but let us judge not, that we be not judged."

But, he insisted, if God wanted to rid the world of American slavery, it might not be surprising that he chose a long and bloody war to do it. Although everyone hoped the war would end soon, it was nevertheless a way for those who had perpetuated and allowed slavery to understand the suffering it had created: "Yet, if God wills that it continue until all the wealth piled by the bondsman's two hundred and fifty years of unrequited toil shall be sunk, and until every drop of blood drawn by the lash shall be paid by another drawn with the sword, as was said three thousand years ago, so still it must be said, 'The judgments of the Lord are true and righteous altogether.'"

Then he went on to an emotional conclusion, replete with "nation's wounds" and "widows and orphans," which has gained a place in America's most famous speeches:

With malice toward none; with charity for all; with firmness in the right, as God gives us to see the right, let us strive on to finish the work we are in; to bind up the nation's wounds; to care for him who shall have borne the battle, and for his widow, and his orphan—to do all which may achieve and cherish a just and lasting peace among ourselves, and with all nations.

The full text of the speech (which is quite short as Presidential inaugural addresses go) is in the appendix.

Rhetoric Is Reformed Out of Existence

During the Middle Ages, rhetoric's foremost figure was St. Augustine, who dealt with persuasion in *De Doctrina Christiana*, in a chapter called "The Christian Orator," written in 426 A.D. Augustine clearly shows a suspicion of rhetoric when he protests that there is nothing sinful about teaching it, and that it is actually useful in counteracting those who would use it to persuade people away from the truth:

Since, then, the faculty of eloquence is available for both sides, and is of very great service in the enforcing either of wrong or right, why do not good men study to engage it on the side of truth, when bad men use it to obtain the triumph of wicked and worthless causes, and to further injustice and error?

Plato could not have written it any better. Augustine went on to explain there are three styles of rhetoric:

- subdued (used for instruction)
- elegant (used for praise)
- majestic (used for exhortation).

All styles, he said, have the same goal: to bring truth to the audience. And that's where rhetoric stood for the next thousand years.

When universities grew up in Medieval Europe, they treated persuasion as one of the liberal arts to be mastered by any educated man. But then again, education was not a very important quality in a man until the Renaissance and the invention of the printing press together worked a revolution in intellectual life.

In the 16th century, Renaissance scholars staged an attack on rhetoric that turned out to all but eliminate it as a field of study. You will remember the five fields of rhetorical study described the Romans:

- invention (finding something to say)
- arrangement (ordering the points of the presentation)
- style (expressing ideas artfully)
- memory (more than memorization, memory also includes strategies for mentally storing a presentation and for making it memorable to the audience)
- delivery (the Greeks called it hypokrisis, or "acting").

The Renaissance scholars said that the first three of these—invention, arrangement, and style—were more properly part of logic or philosophy. That left rhetoric with two fields of study: memory and delivery. But the printing press had been in use for a hundred years by the time the scholars proposed this reform, and the explosive growth of printing had marginalized the skills of memory (in much the same way electronic calculators have marginalized the skills of arithmetic in our own day).

By the time the Renaissance scholars were done, rhetoric had only one field of study: delivery. For the next 400 years, rhetoric was largely whittled down to the study of metaphors and other figures of speech.

The 20th Century and the New Rhetoric

At the turn of the 20th century, the concept of mass communication (in the forms of advertising, entertainment, and propaganda) began to reawaken widespread interest in the concept of persuasion.

New techniques of propaganda and advertising in the early 20th century seemed to make the question of what constitutes persuasiveness more urgent. Scholars have tried to understand the role of context, intention, and convention in communication, and the academic study of rhetoric has become a philosophical enterprise.

As the academics have searched to understand why rhetoric does what it does, business professionals the world over have continued to attempt mastery of the tools of persuasion. And by the 20th century, public speaking had acquired a new companion: visual aids. Both still photography and motion pictures were developed in the 19th century, but their influence on the science of persuasion was not felt until the 20th, when they became less expensive and more flexible and available.

Visual aids substantially increase the ability of persuaders because they open an additional channel of communication to the audience. When objects, events, and processes are shown as well as described, the audience has another way of thinking about the topic. But it's not just a case of illustration. When you present content both verbally and visually—a technique called media redundancy—it seems to help an audience process information.

Modern audiences rarely hear speeches unaccompanied by visuals. Even staged political events, such as conventions, which have a long history of oratory, generally back up speeches with slide shows, films, and video. In the business world, most presenters would not even consider giving a presentation without computer-based slides. Have visual aids improved the ability of persuaders? They have certainly made it easier for someone to hold an audience's interest. But it's important to keep in mind that persuasion usually takes place between people and that the most important prop a presenter can apply is herself. An audience judges slides only incidentally. Its primary goal is to judge the person presenting them. Persuasion takes place when that judgment is favorable, and that may be the most important point in this book.

PART VI
Appendices

The Principles of Persuasion

PRINCIPLE #1
Every point of view is reasonable to the person who holds it.

PRINCIPLE #2
Persuasion does not result from argument or debate.

PRINCIPLE #3
A persuasion event begins long before
you utter a single word.

PRINCIPLE #4
Persuasion takes place in the mind and feelings of the
persuaded, not the persuader.

PRINCIPLE #5
The more communication channels a persuader uses to convey
the message, the greater the chance persuasion will take place.

PRINCIPLE #6
Persuasion requires a persuader; visuals can never do more than
support a persuasion event.

PRINCIPLE #7
Successful persuasion depends on the audience's
trust in the persuader.

PRINCIPLE #8
A persuasive message must be memorable, active, or meaningful.

PRINCIPLE #9
Persuasion never occurs when the persuasion
message is unclear.

Great Moments in Persuasion

This appendix includes a number of public domain speeches, some of which remain among the most persuasive ever made. You will probably find that they all conform to the basic strategy of opening with an appeal to character, making a case through reason, and closing with an appeal to emotion again. But as you read them, you may see that some even use the original six-part plan laid out by Cicero, which we paraphrase here:

1. This is who I am and why I'm here	Character
2. This is the situation we face	Reason
3. This is the goal of the speech	Reason
4. Here is the proof	Reason
5. Here is how someone might try to refute me	Reason
6. This is my concluding statement	Emotion

Patrick Henry "Liberty or Death" Speech

Patrick Henry delivered his famous speech at the Virginia Convention, March 23, 1775. Henry was not a particularly well-educated man, but his education at least extended to Cicero's writings on rhetoric, because this speech is a classic example of Cicero's six-part template. Notice that the first three parts are given in the first paragraph. On the other hand, Henry is quite innovative, because while Cicero suggested that parts two through five should be appeals to reason, virtually everything in this speech is laden with emotion. In that way, it foreshadows much of modern rhetoric.

No man thinks more highly than I do of the patriotism, as well as abilities, of the very worthy gentlemen who have just addressed the House. But different men often see the same subject in different lights; and, therefore, I hope it will not be thought disrespectful to those gentlemen if, entertaining as I do opinions of a character very opposite to theirs, I shall speak forth my sentiments freely and without reserve. This is no time for ceremony. The questing before the House is one of awful moment to this country. For my own part, I consider it as nothing less than a question of freedom or slavery; and in proportion to the magnitude of the subject ought to be the freedom of the debate. It is only in this way that we can hope to arrive at truth, and fulfill the great responsibility which we hold to God and our country. Should I keep back my opinions at such a time, through fear of giving offense, I should consider myself as guilty of treason towards my country, and of an act of disloyalty toward the Majesty of Heaven, which I revere above all earthly kings.

Mr. President, it is natural to man to indulge in the illusions of hope. We are apt to shut our eyes against a painful truth, and listen to the song of that siren till she transforms us into beasts. Is this the part of wise men, engaged in a great and arduous struggle for liberty? Are we disposed to be of the number of those who, having eyes, see not, and, having ears, hear not, the things which so nearly concern their temporal salvation? For my part, whatever anguish of spirit it may cost, I am willing to know the whole truth; to know the worst, and to provide for it.

I have but one lamp by which my feet are guided, and that is the lamp of experience. I know of no way of judging of the future but by the past. And judging by the past, I wish to know what there has been in the conduct of the British ministry for the last ten years to justify those hopes with which gentlemen have been pleased to solace themselves and the House. Is it that insidious smile with which our petition has been lately received? Trust it not, sir; it will prove a snare to your feet. Suffer not yourselves to be betrayed with a kiss. Ask yourselves how this gracious reception of our petition comports with those warlike preparations which cover our waters and darken our land. Are fleets and armies necessary to a work of love and reconciliation? Have we shown ourselves so unwilling to be reconciled that force must be called in to win back our love? Let us not deceive ourselves, sir. These are the implements of war and subjugation; the last arguments to which kings resort. I ask gentlemen, sir, what means this martial array, if its purpose be not to force us to submission? Can gentlemen assign any other possible motive for it? Has Great Britain any enemy, in this quarter of the world, to call for all this accumulation of navies and armies? No, sir, she has none. They are meant for us: they can be meant for no other. They are sent over to bind and rivet upon us those chains which the British ministry have been so long forging. And what have we to oppose to them? Shall we try argument? Sir, we have been trying that for the last ten years. Have we anything new to offer upon the subject? Nothing. We have held the subject up in every light of which it is capable; but it has been all in vain. Shall we resort to entreaty and humble supplication? What terms shall we find which have not been already exhausted? Let us not, I beseech you, sir, deceive ourselves. Sir, we have done everything that could be done to avert the storm which is now coming on. We have petitioned; we have remonstrated; we have supplicated; we have prostrated ourselves before the throne, and have implored its interposition to arrest the tyrannical hands of the ministry and Parliament. Our petitions have been slighted; our remonstrances have produced additional violence and insult; our supplications have been disregarded; and we have been spurned, with contempt, from the foot of the throne! In vain, after these things, may we indulge the fond hope of peace and reconciliation. There is no longer any room for hope. If we wish to be free—if we mean to preserve inviolate those inestimable privileges for which we have been so long contending—if we mean not basely to abandon the noble struggle in which we have been so long engaged, and which we have pledged ourselves never to abandon until the glorious object of our contest shall be obtained—we must fight! I repeat it, sir, we must fight! An appeal to arms and to the God of hosts is all that is left us!

They tell us, sir, that we are weak; unable to cope with so formidable an adversary. But when shall we be stronger? Will it be the next week, or the next year? Will it be when we are totally disarmed, and when a British guard shall be stationed in every house? Shall we gather strength by irresolution and inaction? Shall we acquire the means of effectual resistance by lying supinely on our backs and hugging the delusive phantom of hope, until our enemies shall have bound us hand and foot? Sir, we are not weak if we make a proper use of those means which the God of nature hath placed in our power. The millions of people, armed in the holy cause of liberty, and in such a country as that which we possess, are invincible by any force which our enemy can send against us. Besides, sir, we shall not fight our battles alone. There is a just God who presides over the destinies of nations, and who will raise up friends to fight our battles for us. The battle, sir, is not to the strong alone; it is to the vigilant, the active, the brave. Besides, sir, we have no election. If we were base enough to desire it, it is now too late to retire from the contest. There is no retreat but in submission and slavery! Our chains are forged! Their clanking may be heard on the plains of Boston! The war is inevitable—and let it come! I repeat it, sir, let it come.

It is in vain, sir, to extenuate the matter. Gentlemen may cry, Peace, Peace—but there is no peace. The war is actually begun! The next gale that sweeps from the north will bring to our ears the clash of resounding arms! Our brethren are already in the field! Why stand we here idle? What is it that gentlemen wish? What would they have? Is life so dear, or peace so sweet, as to be purchased at the price of chains and slavery? Forbid it, Almighty God! I know not what course others may take; but as for me, give me liberty or give me death!

Project Gutenberg Etext #6
http://www.gutenberg.net/etext/6

Susan B. Anthony "Right to Suffrage" Speech

Susan B. Anthony delivered this famous speech in 1873, after her arrest and trial for voting in the presidential election of 1872. It helps to know a little of the circumstances surrounding her arrest. Anthony had been an activist in the cause of women's rights ever since she was refused permission to speak at a temperance meeting in Albany in 1852. She was a tireless advocate and, after more than a decade of chairing different associations championing the abolition of slavery and protecting the rights of women, she became the publisher of the newspaper Revolution *in 1868. She co-founded the National Women's Suffrage Association in 1869, and the next year she left her position with* Revolution *to embark on a speaking tour to raise money to pay off the newspaper's debts. After she was arrested for voting in the presidential election in 1872, the judge wrote the directed verdict of guilty before the trial began. The court fined her, but she refused to pay and no action was ever taken against her. The speech she made about her conviction has long outlived in the public imagination the written opinion of the judge who convicted her!*

It shall be my work this evening to prove to you that in thus voting, I not only committed no crime, but, instead, simply exercised my citizen's rights, guaranteed to me and all United States citizens by the National Constitution, beyond the power of any State to deny.... The preamble of the Federal Constitution says:

"We, the people of the United States, in order to form a more perfect union, establish justice, insure domestic tranquillity, provide for the common defense, promote the general welfare, and secure the blessings of liberty to ourselves and our posterity, do ordain and establish this Constitution for the United States of America."

It was we, the people; not we, the white male citizens; nor yet we, the male citizens; but we, the whole people, who formed the Union. And we formed it, not to give the blessings of liberty, but to secure them; not to the half of ourselves and the half of our posterity, but to the whole people—women as well as men. And it is a downright mockery to talk to women of their enjoyment of the blessings of liberty while they are denied the use of the only means of securing them provided by this democratic-republican government—the ballot.

For any State to make sex a qualification that must ever result in the disfranchisement of one entire half of the people is to pass a bill of attainder, or an ex post facto law, and is therefore a violation of the supreme law of the land. By it the blessings of liberty are for ever withheld from women and their female posterity. To them this government has no just powers derived from the consent of the governed. To them this government is not a democracy. It is not a republic. It is an odious aristocracy; a hateful oligarchy of sex; the most hateful aristocracy ever established on the face of the globe; an oligarchy of wealth, where the rich govern the poor. An oligarchy of learning, where the educated govern the ignorant, or even an oligarchy of race, where the Saxon rules the African, might be endured; but this oligarchy of sex, which makes father, brothers, husband, sons, the oligarchs over the mother and sisters, the wife and daughters of every household—which ordains all men sovereigns, all women subjects, carries dissension, discord and rebellion into every home of the nation.

Webster, Worcester and Bouvier all define a citizen to be a person in the United States, entitled to vote and hold office.

The only question left to be settled now is: Are women persons? And I hardly believe any of our opponents will have the hardihood to say they are not. Being persons, then, women are citizens; and no State has a right to make any law, or to enforce any old law, that shall abridge their privileges or immunities. Hence, every discrimination against women in the constitutions and laws of the several States is today null and void, precisely as is every one against negroes.

The World's Famous Orations. At the website, Bartleby.com.
http://www.bartleby.com/268/10/5.html

Abraham Lincoln's Second Inaugural Address

When Lincoln was inaugurated for his second term as President, he faced a difficult situation. The country was in a civil war that had begun as the suppression of a rebellion and had evolved into a crusade to eliminate slavery. To justify the enormous cost of the war in lives and resources, Lincoln signed the Emancipation Proclamation in 1863. But he now found himself leading a citizenry weary of war and often doubting the value of the antislavery crusade. He had to take every opportunity to renew the country's commitment to it.

His Second Inaugural Address, which is quite short by standards of Presidential Inaugural speeches, conforms closely to the six-part template, especially in its emotional conclusion.

Fellow countrymen: At this second appearing to take the oath of the presidential office, there is less occasion for an extended address than there was at the first. Then a statement, somewhat in detail, of a course to be pursued, seemed fitting and proper. Now, at the expiration of four years, during which public declarations have been constantly called forth on every point and phase of the great contest which still absorbs the attention and engrosses the energies of the nation, little that is new could be presented. The progress of our arms, upon which all else chiefly depends, is as well known to the public as to myself; and it is, I trust, reasonably satisfactory and encouraging to all. With high hope for the future, no prediction in regard to it is ventured.

On the occasion corresponding to this four years ago, all thoughts were anxiously directed to an impending civil war. All dreaded it—all sought to avert it. While the inaugural address was being delivered from this place, devoted altogether to saving the Union without war, insurgent agents were in the city seeking to destroy it without war—seeking to dissolve the Union, and divide effects, by negotiation. Both parties deprecated war; but one of them would make war rather than let the nation survive; and the other would accept war rather than let it perish. And the war came.

One-eighth of the whole population were colored slaves, not distributed generally over the Union, but localized in the Southern part of it. These slaves constituted a peculiar and powerful interest. All knew that this interest was, somehow, the cause of the war. To strengthen, perpetuate, and extend this interest was the object for which the insurgents would rend the Union, even by war; while the government claimed no right to do more than to restrict the territorial enlargement of it.

Neither party expected for the war the magnitude or the duration which it has already attained. Neither anticipated that the cause of the conflict might cease with, or even before, the conflict itself should cease. Each looked for an easier triumph, and a result less fundamental and astounding. Both read the same Bible, and pray to the same God; and each invokes his aid against the other. It may seem strange that any men should dare to ask a just God's assistance in wringing their bread from the sweat of other men's faces; but let us judge not, that we be not judged. The prayers of both could not be answered—that of neither has been answered fully.

The Almighty has his own purposes. "Woe unto the world because of offenses! For it must needs be that offenses come; but woe to that man by whom the offense cometh." If we shall suppose that American slavery is one of those offenses which, in the providence of God, must needs come, but which, having continued through his appointed time, he now wills to remove, and that he gives to both North and South this terrible war, as the woe due to those by whom the offense came, shall we discern therein any departure from those divine attributes which the believers in a living God always ascribe to him? Fondly do we hope—fervently do we pray—that this mighty scourge of war may speedily pass away. Yet, if God wills that it continue until all the wealth piled by the bondsman's two hundred and fifty years of unrequited toil shall be sunk, and until every drop of blood drawn by the lash shall be paid by another drawn with the sword, as was said three thousand years ago, so still it must be said, "The judgments of the Lord are true and righteous altogether."

With malice toward none; with charity for all; with firmness in the right, as God gives us to see the right, let us strive on to finish the work we are in; to bind up the nation's wounds; to care for him who shall have borne the battle, and for his widow, and his orphan—to do all which may achieve and cherish a just and lasting peace among ourselves, and with all nations.

Project Gutenberg Etext #8
http://www.gutenberg.net/etext/8

Red Jacket Answers a Missionary

"Red Jacket" was the English name of Seneca chief Sagoyewatha (1758-1830), who used magnificent oratory to distract his people from knowing he was double-dealing them in land cessions with the Americans. He delivered this speech at the Council of the Six Nations in the Summer of 1805 after a missionary named Cram gave a speech describing the work he intended to do among the Seneca. What is particularly remarkable about this speech is how closely it conforms to Cicero's six-step template, despite Red Jacket's lack of a classical education.

Friend and Brother: It was the will of the Great Spirit that we should meet together this day. He orders all things and has given us a fine day for our council. He has taken His garment from before the sun and caused it to shine with brightness upon us. Our eyes are opened that we see clearly; our ears are unstopped that we have been able to hear distinctly the words you have spoken. For all these favors we thank the Great Spirit, and Him only.

Brother, this council fire was kindled by you. It was at your request that we came together at this time. We have listened with attention to what you have said. You requested us to speak our minds freely. This gives us great joy; for we now consider that we stand upright before you and can speak what we think. All have heard your voice and all speak to you now as one man. Our minds are agreed.

Brother, you say you want an answer to your talk before you leave this place. It is right you should have one, as you are a great distance from home and we do not wish to detain you. But first we will look back a little and tell you what our fathers have told us and what we have heard from the white people.

Brother, listen to what we say. There was a time when our forefathers owned this great island. Their seats extended from the rising to the setting sun. The Great Spirit had made it for the use of Indians. He had created the buffalo, the deer, and other animals for food. He had made the bear and the beaver. Their skins served us for clothing. He had scattered them over the country and taught us how to take them. He had caused the earth to produce corn for bread. All this He had done for His red children because He loved them. If we had some disputes about our hunting-ground they were generally settled without the shedding of much blood.

But an evil day came upon us. Your forefathers crossed the great water and landed on this island. Their numbers were small. They found friends and not enemies. They told us they had fled from their own country for fear of wicked men and had come here to enjoy their religion. They asked for a small seat. We took pity on them, granted their request, and they sat down among us. We gave them corn and meat; they gave us poison in return.

The white people, brother, had now found our country. Tidings were carried back and more came among us. Yet we did not fear them. We took them to be friends. They called us brothers. We believed them and gave them a larger seat. At length their numbers had greatly increased. They wanted more land; they wanted our country. Our eyes were opened and our minds became uneasy. War took place. Indians were hired to fight against Indians, and many of our people were destroyed. They also brought strong liquor among us. It was strong and powerful, and has slain thousands.

Brother, our seats were once large and yours were small. You have now become a great people, and we have scarcely a place left to spread our blankets. You have got our country, but are not satisfied; you want to force your religion upon us.

Brother, continue to listen. You say that you are sent to instruct us how to worship the Great Spirit agreeably to His mind; and, if we do not take hold of the religion which you white people teach we shall be unhappy hereafter. You say that you are right and we are lost. How do we know this to be true? We understand that your religion is written in a Book. If it was intended for us, as well as you, why has not the Great Spirit given to us, and not only to us, but why did He not give to our forefathers the knowledge of that Book, with the means of understanding it rightly. We only know what you tell us about it. How shall we know when to believe, being so often deceived by the white people?

Brother, you say there is but one way to worship and serve the Great Spirit. If there is but one religion, why do you white people differ so much about it? Why not all agreed, as you can all read the Book.

Brother, we do not understand these things. We are told that your religion was given to your forefathers and has been handed down from father to son. We also have a religion which was given to our forefathers and has been handed down to us, their children. We worship in that way. It teaches us to be thankful for all the favors we receive, to love each other, and to be united. We never quarrel about religion.

Brother, the Great Spirit has made us all, but He has made a great difference between His white and His red children. He has given us different complexions and different customs. To you He has given the arts. To these He has not opened our eyes. We know these things to be true. Since He has made so great a difference between us in other things, why may we not conclude that He has given us a different religion according to our understanding? The Great Spirit does right. He knows what is best for His children; we are satisfied.

Brother, we do not wish to destroy your religion or take it from you. We only want to enjoy our own.

Brother, you say you have not come to get our land or our money, but to enlighten our minds. I will now tell you that I have been at your meetings and saw you collect money from the meeting. I can not tell what this money was intended for, but suppose that it was for your minister; and, if we should conform to your way of thinking, perhaps you may want some from us.

Brother, we are told that you have been preaching to the white people in this place. These people are our neighbors. We are acquainted with them. We will wait a little while and see what effect your preaching has upon them. If we find it does them good, makes them honest, and less disposed to cheat Indians, we will then consider again of what you have said.

Brother, you have now heard our answer to your talk, and this is all we have to say at present. As we are going to part, we will come and take you by the hand, and hope the Great Spirit will protect you on your journey and return you safe to your friends.

The World's Famous Orations. At the website Bartleby.com.
http://www.bartleby.com/268/8/3.html

John F. Kennedy "Ich bin ein Berliner"

On June 26, 1963, in the wake of worldwide nervousness about the American-Soviet confrontation over missles in Cuba, President John F. Kennedy gave a speech in the city of Berlin. Berlin was then surrounded by Soviet occupation, and Kennedy went to Berlin both as a dramatic gesture of defiance and to reassure the population there that the United States would stand with them for freedom. The speech he gave reassured the Berliners sufficiently that the city was wracked with riots for days afterward—a case study in surpassing a persuasive goal!

Because "Berliner" is the name of a jelly doughnut in colloquial German, it is widely believed that Kennedy's famous phrase amounted to "I am a jelly doughnut," and that the audience laughed at him for it. This is an urban legend. It is true that "Berliner" means jelly doughnut in German, but only outside Berlin. In the city, the word for jelly doughnut is "Pfannkuchen." The preferred usage would have been "Ich bin Berliner" (without the article), but the crowd understood him perfectly well. The only laughter you can hear in the audio recordings of the speech occurs when Kennedy's translator repeated the phrase "Ich bin ein Berliner" and Kennedy, a legendary wit, ironically thanked him for translating his German.

I am proud to come to this city as the guest of your distinguished Mayor, who has symbolized throughout the world the fighting spirit of West Berlin. And I am proud to visit the Federal Republic with your distinguished Chancellor who for so many years has committed Germany to democracy and freedom and progress, and to come here in the company of my fellow American, General Clay, who has been in this city during its great moments of crisis and will come again if ever needed.

Two thousand years ago the proudest boast was *"civis Romanus sum."* Today, in the world of freedom, the proudest boast is *"Ich bin ein Berliner."*

I appreciate my interpreter translating my German!

There are many people in the world who really don't understand, or say they don't, what is the great issue between the free world and the Communist world. Let them come to Berlin. There are some who say that communism is the wave of the future. Let them come to Berlin. And there are some who say in Europe and elsewhere we can work with the Communists. Let them come to Berlin. And there are even a few who say that it is true that communism is an evil system, but it permits us to make economic progress. *Lass' sie nach Berlin kommen.* Let them come to Berlin.

Freedom has many difficulties and democracy is not perfect, but we have never had to put a wall up to keep our people in, to prevent them from leaving us. I want to say, on behalf of my countrymen, who live many miles away on the other side of the Atlantic, who are far distant from you, that they take the greatest pride that they have been able to share with you, even from a distance, the story of the last 18 years. I know of no town, no city, that has been besieged for 18 years that still lives with the vitality and the force, and the hope and the determination of the city of West Berlin. While the wall is the most obvious and vivid demonstration of the failures of the Communist system, for all the world to see, we take no satisfaction in it, for it is, as your Mayor has said, an offense not only against history but an offense against humanity, separating families, dividing husbands and wives and brothers and sisters, and dividing a people who wish to be joined together.

What is true of this city is true of Germany—real, lasting peace in Europe can never be assured as long as one German out of four is denied the elementary right of free men, and that is to make a free choice. In 18 years of peace and good faith, this generation of Germans has earned the right to be free, including the right to unite their families and their nation in lasting peace, with good will to all people. You live in a defended island of freedom, but your life is part of the main. So let me ask you as I close, to lift your eyes beyond the dangers of today, to the hopes of tomorrow, beyond the freedom merely of this city of Berlin, or your country of Germany, to the advance of freedom everywhere, beyond the wall to the day of peace with justice, beyond yourselves and ourselves to all mankind.

Freedom is indivisible, and when one man is enslaved, all are not free. When all are free, then we can look forward to that day when this city will be joined as one and this country and this great Continent of Europe in a peaceful and hopeful globe. When that day finally comes, as it will, the people of West Berlin can take sober satisfaction in the fact that they were in the front lines for almost two decades.

All free men, wherever they may live, are citizens of Berlin, and, therefore, as a free man, I take pride in the words *"Ich bin ein Berliner."*

"Remarks in the Rudolph Wilde Platz," John F. Kennedy Library and Museum.
http://www.jfklibrary.org/j062663.htm

APPENDIX C

Sources

"Actor Garner Gives $500G to Univ. of Okla.," *AP Online*, April 4, 2003.

"Active Listening," *Public Management*, December 1, 1997.

Allen, Crystal. "It's Almost Like Being There," *Christian Science Monitor*, July 14, 2004.

Anthony, Susan Brownell. "On Woman's Right to the Suffrage." *The World's Famous Orations*. At the website, *Bartleby.com*. http://www.bartleby.com/268/10/5.html

Bartlett, John (Justin Kaplan, general editor). *Bartlett's Familiar Quotations*, 17th edition, Little, Brown and Company, 2002.

Bonaparte, Napoleon. "To His Soldiers at Fontainebleau." *The World's Famous Orations*. At the website, *Bartleby.com*. http://www.bartleby.com/268/7/34.html

Bonaparte, Napoleon. "To the Army in Italy." *The World's Famous Orations*. At the website, *Bartleby.com*. http://www.bartleby.com/268/7/29.html

Boyle, Matthew. "Speech Therapy," *Fortune*, August 13, 2001.

Brockman, John. "'The Thing that I Call Doug': A Talk with Douglas Rushkoff," *Edge*, October 25, 1999 (Web publication at: http://www.edge.org/documents/archive/edge61.html)

Bruzzese, Anita. "Small Group Presentations Carry Own Set of Issues," Gannett News Service, May 29, 2003.

Burton, Gideon O. *Silva Rhetoricae* website at
http://humanities.byu.edu/rhetoric/silva.htm

Clough, A.H., editor. *Plutarch's Lives*, Project Gutenberg Etext #674

Craddock, Richard Cameron. "The New Rhetoric." At the website,
Rhetoric Resources, maintained by the School of Literature,
Communication, and Culture of Georgia Institute of Technology.
http://www.lcc.gatech.edu/gallery/rhetoric/issues/newrhetoric.html

David, Amelia. "Strategies for Coping with Stage Fright and Stress,"
Back Stage, June 29, 2001.

Goldstein, Alan. "Meeting Participants Need to Mind Manners Even in
Virtual Settings," *Dallas Morning News*, January 7, 2003.

Kennedy, John F. "Remarks in the Rudolph Wilde Platz." John F.
Kennedy Library and Museum. Web page at
http://www.jfklibrary.org/j062663.htm

Kitchen, Patricia. "Conquering Fear of Public Speaking," *Newsday*,
November 21, 1999.

Lawren, Bill. "Seating for Success," *Psychology Today*, September 1, 1989.

Lewis, Edward and Myers, Robert, eds. *A Treasury of Mark Twain*,
Hallmark Editions, 1967.

Lincoln, Abraham. "Second Inaugural Address," Project Gutenberg
Etext #8

Markel, Mike. "Testing visual-based modules for teaching writing,"
Technical Communication, February 1, 1998.

Meetings in America V: Meeting of the Minds, an MCI Executive White
Paper (2003). Website: http://e-meetings.mci.com/meetingsinameri-
ca/pdf/MIA5.pdf

Mehrabian, Albert. *Nonverbal Communication*, Aldine-Atherton, 1972.
Merritt, Mark. "Taming the Beast Within: 6 Coaches Share their
Secrets for Conquering Speaking Anxiety," *Presentations*, March 1, 2002.
Peterson, Pat. "How to Execute an Integrated Campaign," Panel dis-
cussion, New England Direct Marketing Association 2004 Conference,
June 18, 2004.

Petraglia-Bahri, Joseph. "A Brief Overview of Rhetoric." At the website *Rhetoric Resources*, maintained by the School of Literature,
Communication, and Culture of Georgia Institute of Technology.
http://www.lcc.gatech.edu/gallery/rhetoric/essay.html

Postma, Albert. "Inter- and Intramodal Encoding of Auditory and
Visual Presentation of Material: Effects on Memory Performance,"
The Psychological Record, June 22, 2000.

"Public Speaking Tests the Nerves of Most Directors,"
The Birmingham Post, August 25, 2003.

Rushkoff, Douglas. Coercion: *Why We Listen to What "They" Say*,
Riverhead Books, 1999.

Tomlinson, Edward C. and Lewicki, Roy J. "Trust and Trust Building,"
at the website *Beyond Intractability.org*
(www.beyondintractability.org/m/trust_building.jsp).

Tracy, Larry. "How 'Fear of Speaking' Can Make You a Better
Speaker." Web page at http://www.web-source.net/web_develop-
ment/public_speaking.htm

"Rhetoric" in *Wikipedia*, the free encyclopedia. Web page at
http://en.wikipedia.org/wiki/Rhetoric

About Communispond

COMMUNISPOND was founded in 1969. Today, almost 35 years later, it is the resource of choice when there's a lot riding on how well you communicate.

At Communispond, we believe that improving communication skills improves business. And we've proved it over and over again with thousands of clients in the U.S. and around the world. Our services have been sought out by hundreds of board chairmen and company presidents and tens of thousands of sales executives, not to mention world champion athletes, media figures and candidates for high office.

Communispond has helped clients prepare for many different types of communication situations, such as corporate merger and reorganization announcements, new sales pitches, crucial new product launches, liability and recall disclosures, appeals to government regulatory bodies, communication with Wall Street and shareholders, press conferences and media interviews, announcements affecting employee benefits and job security, efforts to unite employees around a common mission. And of course, we work with companies on their daily communication issues, helping intact teams work better, fostering communication between managers and subordinates, or improving performance appraisal and other coaching discussions.

We're known worldwide for our Executive Presentation Skills program, but we've expanded beyond presentation skills to offer a broad range of solutions addressing virtually every communications discipline; business writing skills, facilitation skills, listening skills, even how to master today's new virtual communications channels. What's more, you may now tap Communispond for any population that must hold their own in high stakes communications situations, including

- Sales forces battling to beat quota and increase market share
- Marketing departments launching new products and services
- Technical teams managing mission-critical projects
- Leaders instigating change

Today, after 35 years of research and field trials, Communispond offer a comprehensive suite of solutions to help your key people deliver the right message to the right audience in the right way. Our clients include 350 of the Fortune 500 and Communispond "graduates" number more than 500,000 individuals, representing industry leaders all over the globe.

About the Authors

KEVIN DALEY founded Communispond in 1969. At that time he was a Vice President and Management Supervisor for The J. Walter Thompson Company, the world's largest advertising agency.

Effective presentations were the lifeblood of the advertising business and Kevin was intent on creating a program to improve the presentation skills of the officers of JWT, in order to make them more effective, dynamic speakers in front of any audience. The program was so successful that it was offered to clients and then to the business community at large.

Kevin has personally trained 62 Board Chairmen, 320 company Presidents, and 3100 sales managers. He is also a sought-after speaker by business groups around the world.

Kevin is the author of two previous top-selling business books. *Talk Your Way to the Top* outlines how to address any audience as though your career depended on it. *Socratic Selling* teaches salespeople to build stronger relationships with clients and prospects by improving dialoging and communication skills.

Kevin is a graduate of Fordham University and is a former U.S. Navy jet pilot, who has never outgrown the thrill of landing on aircraft carriers. He is a former President of the Instructional Systems Association, a training industry group comprised of 130 of the best-known training companies. He lives with his family in Greenwich, Connecticut.

PAM ERB-MELVILLE is a Master Instructor and Executive Coach for Communispond.

She is a specialist in the core Communispond Programs, including those addressing presentation skills, sales communication, dialogue skills, business writing, and coaching.

Pam also specializes in one-on-one Executive Coaching, helping her clients improve their presentation skills. Those she coaches leave the experience with new skills and an inspired enthusiasm to use them in both their professional and personal lives.

Pam received a master's degree in Speech/Theatre from Bowling Green State University and was graduated with Distinction from

Otterbein College in Ohio. She toured with the National Shakespeare Company, performed off-Broadway, in soap operas, and in TV and radio commercials. Pam also traveled throughout the US and Canada as a spokesperson and presenter for Pepsi USA.

Pam is also a small business owner, having founded Bravo New York, a company that provides tour-guide services to inbound groups visiting the Big Apple.

Pam resides in Cobble Hill, Brooklyn with her husband David. She spends her free time improving the distance of her drive and the precision of her putt on any golf course she can find.

WAYNE TURMEL is the National Director of Faculty for Communispond, responsible for the recruiting, training, and management of its faculty.

Wayne is also an exceptional classroom facilitator, specializing in the areas of live and virtual presentation skills, business writing, and supervisory communication. He has taught programs and designed custom training solutions for clients as diverse as IBM, the US Postal Service, Fidelity Capital and Kaiser Permanente.

Wayne has an extensive background in sales and has worked with project teams in the IT and marketing areas.

In addition to his duties for Communispond, he is a well-known writer and speaker in the training industry. His work has appeared in the ASTD Handbook of Instructional Technology, the American Management Association's Handbook on E-Learning, and numerous magazines and newspapers. His first book, *A Philistine's Journal—an Average Guy Tackles the Classics*, was rated one of the top new non-fiction books of 2003 by several reviewers.

DIANE BIEGERT is a Master Instructor and Executive Coach at Communispond. Diane has an extensive background in education, sales, and instructional design. She delivers thirteen of Communispond's eighteen training programs and has designed custom training for numerous clients. She also works one-on-one with senior executives from major corporations, coaching them on communication and presentation skills. Since joining Communispond in 1995 Diane has worked with a myriad of clients across all industries.

Diane graduated from Miami University, Oxford, Ohio with a B.S. in education. Prior to joining Communispond, Diane taught elementary and special education and then sold printing for a major printing company. She was President of Biegert Consulting, Inc., a firm that specialized in facilitating and developing hands-on training workshops for the printing, paper, and publishing industries. Her first book, *Nine Steps to Effective and Efficient Press OKs*, was published by the Graphic Arts Technical Foundation in 2002.

A native of Kansas, Diane now lives in Chicago, Illinois.

LEE VELTA is the National Director of Executive Coaching, overseeing the cadre of coaches who deliver Communispond's individualized training services.

Lee has coached top executives in all aspects of communication and presentation skills. He has prepared CEOs for annual meetings, coached entrepreneurs before their IPO road shows, trained executives to face the media, and even prepared witnesses for courtroom appearances.

Lee joined Communispond in 1993 as a senior faculty member. He has also designed many custom training programs. Lee has worked with clients in many industries, including technology, advertising, pharmaceutical, healthcare, and finance. He has contributed articles to sales and management publications.

Besides a Bachelors of Science, he earned a Masters degree in classical vocal performance from the Conservatory of Music in San Francisco. He has sung with opera companies and symphonies internationally, has appeared on television and radio, and has made three recordings.

Lee has many personal interests, but mostly enjoys concertizing with his wife, soprano Sherry Overholt, being with his new daughter, Olivia, and instructing at the Tai Chi Chuan Center of New York.